1-31-07

I pray
come a

MW01610021

God Bless you

Unleashing the Blessings of God in your Life

by Daryl A. Tate

A More Excellent Way
A STUDY SERIES GUIDE

Printed in the United States of
America

Printing by Global Group Inc.
4901 North Beach Street
Fort Worth, Texas 76137-3498
Cover Design by Marsha Alvey

Acknowledgement

To God be the Glory!
Thank you, Jesus!

. . . and yet show I unto you
a more excellent way.

I Corinthians 12:31

Contents

Preface

Far too long before coming to Christ, my life was superfluous with emptiness and lack. It was not my present task that I was afraid of as much as it was my past failures holding me hostage. Every time I gathered the courage to advance, the enemy met me at the threshold of victory with the consequences of failure. It was my relationship with Christ that finally broke this cycle of ineptitude and revealed to me that the weapon being used against me resonated within me. It was "selfish ambitions," the very contradiction of God's will — a spirit so subverted and deceptive that it can blind one from seeing the true pathway to one's blessings.

To understand the principles in this book, you do not have to be a Harvard professor or a deep thinker, nor do you need to be a spiritual giant or an eloquent speaker. It is not necessary to jump, shout, and break into a dance. God's principles are so simple that they are profound. You need only apply them. Simply *apply*.

Even now, begin to unveil your heart to the Lord. Allow Him to see that you are allowing Him to see where you are. "Adam, where art thou?" the

Lord said to Adam after his transgression in the Garden — not physically, but spiritually. Have you done something to relocate yourself from the vein of God's blessings? God, in the midst of our intense struggles and pressures, will ask us questions that will cause us to search some of the comatose places in our soul, not because He doesn't know the answer, but rather to stir our soul for self-evaluation. Anything that God does is blessed. It is not necessary to beg Him to bless you. Simply find where He is. Are you hiding behind the "fig leaves" of past hurts, bad habits, poor stewardship, or generational curses, when the safety and blessings of God are in walking in His principles? Has the chilly frost of tradition waxed your heart so cold that you have forgotten the deep warmth of God's love?

Well, God has repeatedly spoken to me regarding writing the vision down on tables, that he may run that readeth it. For the vision is yet for an appointed time, but in the end it shall speak, and not lie. (Habakkuk 2:3) The vision that God has given me in its most simple form is for people to know that God's way is A MORE EXCELLENT WAY. Regardless of your race, past, or social classification, God is no respecter of persons. No matter what demographic you fall in, God's principles hold true. If you apply them and are willing and obedient, you will prosper.

What is Prosperity?

Beloved, I wish above all things that thou mayest prosper and be in health, even as thy soul prospereth. 3 John 1:2

God wants His people to walk in His blessings. Note that blessings do not necessarily denote material wealth. Friend, don't misconstrue the two. True prosperity from God will not occur outside of our soul prospering. True prosperity cannot be measured by a standard of comparison to others, but rather by the standard in which the Lord promises according to His Word and His will for each and every one of OUR lives. Not everyone will be blessed the same in a natural or spiritual way. However, whatever the measure meted out to you, if you are in obedience to the will of God in your life, you will be complete, whole, and without lack. You will also bear the fruitful spiritual, emotional, and mental dividends in YOUR life, unmatched by others. Why? Because what God has for you is for you.

Some will be like Abraham, "The Father of Faith." Abraham was very wealthy in substance. If we are not careful, it is easy to question those that have been blessed with great substance. A requisite element is that God gave Abraham his wealth. He did not seek wealth; it was given to him for his faith and obedience to God. (Genesis 22:18) Not only was Abraham blessed naturally, but it was his affluence of faith in God that retrieved his wealth. In contrast, let's look at the widow that gave the two mites. (Mark 12:41–44) Though she did not have much, what she gave was from her heart. This woman may have never been blessed with great substance; however, she was very rich in faith. Her giving is an indication that she understood from whom her blessings flowed. Most Christians fall somewhere in between the substance of Abraham and that of the widow woman. Again, true prosperity is not in substance, one way or the other. It can only be found in your FAITH in His Word and your OBEDIENCE to His will.

You can be the least blessed naturally and extremely blessed spiritually. Let me caution you, though; being the least blessed naturally does not automatically equate to being spiritually blessed, nor does being blessed naturally mean that you are spiritually impoverished. We must take God out of the preconceived borders of our finite mind and remember that with Him all things are possible. (Matthew 19:26) The prosperity that John speaks of is being fruitful. Whatever measure given to you is enough to bring forth blessings. For so long, I've seen Christians "just serving time" here on earth like an inmate does in prison, waiting for a chariot to swing low. That's not living. That's not walking in the newness of life and the promises of God. I often see Christians with an abundance of faith, frustrated because they do not see the movement of God in their lives because they are unprincipled. We must now exercise our faith in the authority of His principles to receive His promises. Understand that it's not enough to just believe. It must be according to His Word. God is not backing up "OUR" belief system. He is backing up OUR FAITH IN HIS WORD — not just those scriptures that are convenient for us to quote that speak about receiving His blessings, but those that also hold us accountable for doing what is required of us. Just as the body without the spirit is dead, so faith without works is dead also. (James 2:26)

Listen here: just God breathing on you is more powerful than hearing hundreds of sermons or reading volumes of books. This book will hopefully increase your faith and inspire you into action. **You**, however, must apply and take action. You must have the experience for yourself. If not, it will only be words versing pages in a book — someone else's testimony. God wants to show **you** something. Let Him change your trials from making it until payday to making a payroll for others.

Often times it is difficult to see God because barriers are between us and Him that distort our vision; garrisons of bad relationships, past hurts, and scars, or busy schedules hinder us from establishing a relationship with Him. Let's begin the overdue journey down the summoning road to *Unleashing the Blessings of God in Your Life* by doing things God's way, A More Excellent Way.

Chapter One

A More Excellent Way

A more excellent way does not replace God's way; it defines it, because God IS Excellence. For the believer, there is only one excellent way — that is God's way, in everything.

od anoints our lives so that He can be the driving force that keeps us moving forward in a positive and effective direction. Not the world's way, but His way, the more excellent way — business, ministry, worship, finances, everything the more excellent way. It is imperative to learn God's way as a parent, spouse, employee, boss, entrepreneur, minister, or whatever your profession may be. Problems in these primary areas of our lives are really consequences of not doing things in a more excellent way in areas that seem translucent.

Because of this, we experience a vicious cycle of cause and effect, unfruitfulness, that leaves us frustrated, confused, and defeated. We must break the cycle of inferiority that feeds our complacency to mediocrity. The challenge of modifying these holding patterns of life into a course navigated for success must not be perceived merely as a project, but rather as a **process**. A **process** of transformation by the renewing of the mind.

In the private schools that I attended growing up, I learned about the Lord, but I was never enlightened to THE MORE EXCELLENT WAY of the power of God. I comprehended that God loved me, but I never experienced how He can deliver, heal, and strengthen me to accomplish His will in my life. I always felt that the Lord was an Icon that sat high and looked low with a very nonchalant perspective toward my life. I believed that He set up commandments of do's and don'ts, and if exemplary behavior outnumbered the derogatory, I would have passed the test of life. I didn't know that even before accepting Him, Jesus was then and is still now interceding for me, praying that my faith does not fail — that He is lobbying with the Father on my behalf. I learned through a relationship with Him that He is poised at the door of my life, waiting to be invited in so that He can handle what I cannot. It is amazing that while I was living in a deceived spiritual state, Christ was advocating more grace to abound in my life to His Father. This grace was manifested in the form of a hedge of safety, while the enemies' onslaught of destructive devices were at work. Many times I've stared down the barrel of a loaded gun with an individual intoxicated enough to pull the trigger and not remember it the next day. Each time, the Lord's grace interceded. The enemy was trying to obliterate me before giving my heart to God. Regardless of my will to shun His Gift of Life, the Lord continued to consign people my way to sow seeds in my heart.

What I am saying is that I believed in God, but I didn't know God. For years I thought that my security would be in getting a college degree and having a good-paying career. You can have more degrees than a thermometer and more money than you can spend, but without God it is vanity. All the while I relentlessly pursued the "things" of the world, the vacuous cavern in my life gaped open wider and wider. You know, the void that God puts in every human creature that only He can fill and fulfill. It is amazing how we run to substance abuse, promiscuity, power, money, bad relationships, and other carnal depravity to fill a spiritual void. It will not happen! Unless you allow the divine power of God to fill you, your void will remain inflamed, and no lust of the flesh will quench it. I pray that as you verse these pages that the anointing and power of God will speak to your heart to give you the desire to choose to live your life God's way, A MORE EXCELLENT WAY.

The Most Excellent Way

That if thou shalt confess with thy mouth the Lord Jesus, and shalt believe in thine heart that God hath raised him from the dead, thou shalt be saved. For with the heart man believeth unto righteousness; and with the mouth confession is made unto salvation. Romans 10:9–10

The most excellent plan ever established was the Lord's plan of SALVATION! Let me add that the most excellent decision that you will ever make in your life is to accept it. If you are reading this book, God is already dealing with your heart. The Holy Spirit is speaking to you right now. Allow Him in, by not closing the door to your heart. Let Him speak to you only the way He can. Go ahead; ask Him if you already haven't. Say "Lord, I am a sinner and I can't help myself. Precious Savior, come into my life and save me. Fill me with Your Spirit." From the day that I spoke those words, my life has never been the same. Sure, I had been to church many times, sang in the choir, even worked in ministry, but I had never asked the Lord for a personal relationship with Him. Therefore if any man *be* in Christ, *he* is a new creature: old things are passed away; behold, all things are become new. (II Corinthians 5:17) To be in Christ, His Spirit must be in you. The Lord fills you with the Holy Spirit and His power when you relinquish and give your life to Him. Note, this passage of scripture does not say if any man be in church, be a deacon, or be in the choir. The stipulation is being in Christ, having a relationship with Him, being faithful to Him. He is the key that unlocks the door to your blessings. Another point made in this passage is that "if **any** man be in Christ . . ." not just some men and excluding others, not just wealthy men, or even poor men. Any man in Christ is a new creature. To begin to under-stand the principles in this book, let alone apply them, you must first be in Christ. You must first develop a relationship with Him that prioritizes Him as number one in your life.

The thief cometh not, but for to steal, and to kill, and to destroy: I am come that they might have life, and that they might have it more abundantly. John 10:10

What I am writing about is not something that I've heard, nor someone else's experience. It is actually the realistic manifestation of the grace of God abounding in my life. You see, I've been there. I've been so intoxicated behind the wheel of a car that I woke up the next morning and checked the front end of my car to make sure that I had not hit someone. This once occurred after leaving a corporate happy hour. I've been $35,000 in consumer debt, while being three months late on my car note, two months late on my rent, and unemployed. I've been there, friend, on the high-speed, nonadvancing treadmill of life — running hard but going nowhere fast. I know what it means to have a deep, incisive yearning to be successful, yet every time you take one step forward, you end up three miles back. I understand never having the power to accomplish a goal in life. I understand the lack of fulfillment. I know the feeling of everything looking good on the outside, but inside there is a feeling of despair. I was exhibiting what I call "**pseudo-excellence**" in my life. That is excellence on the exterior but no substance in my soul. There are many people subscribing to "pseudo-excellence." Motivational practices and theories abound with no foundational teaching on WHO true excellence really is. We try to achieve excellence, but God IS EXCELLENCE. He is the embodiment of the very thing that we are seeking. So tell me, how can you have excellence and leave Him out?

People see me now that I'm walking in the newness of life and His marvelous light and can't imagine that it hasn't always been that way. "You're so blessed and God has placed His anointing on your life," I hear people say. "Praise God" is my response. I do realize, however, that God didn't reach down and lift me up from the depths of my sin for me to seek applause or applaud myself. It was nothing that I can take one iota of credit for. I couldn't help myself. I was dead in the trespasses of sin, but God who is rich in mercy has raised us up together with Christ Jesus. (Ephesians 2:4) God is rich in mercy. What is mercy? Well, what do you need? Do you need healing? But God who is rich in healing . . . Do you need understanding? But God who is rich in wisdom . . . Are you stressed? But God who is rich in peace . . . Depressed? But God who is rich in joy . . . Salvation? But God who is rich in grace . . . Now you're getting it. Mercy means whatever you NEED, God has an abundance of it. All the honor and glory go to Him. Again, why did He do it? He did it so that I could throw out the lifeline to someone else who is hurting and desiring to fill the void in their life that only Almighty God can fill. He did it because He sent

His Son who gave His life so that we might have life and have it more abundantly. He did it for YOU! And He did it for ME. Say that out loud right now. Go ahead; do it. Speak it. Say "Jesus came that I might have life and have it more abundantly (to its fullest measure)." Did you feel something? Say it until you do.

Delight thyself also in the Lord; and he shall give thee the desires of thine heart. **Psalm 37:4**

One of the foremost deceptions that Satan uses when the Lord is dealing with someone's heart is "Look at all of the constraints that you must endure." Well, he did with me anyway. "I'm going to have to be poor, look pitiful, and stop doing everything." Look, friend, it is a deception. I've seen both sides of the spectrum. It is, in fact, the Lord's yoke that is easy and burdens that are light. I've worked for Fortune 1000 companies, making good money, seeking after the riches of the world. I found out that I had enough money to keep my suits cleaned, take a vacation a couple of times a year, and buy a new car every four or five years. That's not the fullness of God's blessings. Let's begin to UNLEASH THE BLESSINGS OF GOD IN YOUR LIFE. Since surrendering my life to Him and applying the principles in His Word, He has given me the desires of my heart.

My family has been blessed with health. He has given me CEO stewardship of three blessed companies. My wife is able to be at home full time to raise our children and run our household. The peace and the joy that He gives, even during difficult times, is priceless. I have never been happier. He wants to do the same thing for YOU! Did you hear me? God wants to bless you. Beloved, I wish above all things, that thou mayest prosper and be in health, even as thy soul prospereth. (III John 1:2) The Lord of lords wants you to be fruitful while you are physically, mentally, emotionally, and spiritually able to enjoy it. There is one prerequisite. He wants it to be in conjunction with your soul being prepared to enter into eternal life. What an awesome love — so great that He won't bless you in this life, only for you to spend eternity in hell.

And You Hath He Quickened . . .

Ephesians 2:1–7
1: And you [hath he quickened], who were dead in trespasses and sins; 2: Wherein in time past ye walked according to the course of this world, according to the prince of the power of the air, the spirit that now worketh in the children of disobedience: 3: Among whom also we all had our conversation in times past in the lusts of our

flesh, fulfilling the desires of the flesh and of the mind; and were by nature the children of wrath, even as others. 4: But God, who is rich in mercy, for his great love wherewith he loved us, 5: Even when we were dead in sins hath quickened us together with Christ, (by grace ye are saved;) 6: And hath raised [us] up together, and made [us] sit together in heavenly [places] in Christ Jesus. 7: That in the ages to come he might show the exceeding riches of his grace, in [his] kindness toward us through Jesus Christ.

In February of 1994, I received a call stating that my grandfather was terminally ill with cancer and had only two or three days to live. My wife and I loaded our minivan for the trip from Dallas to Chicago. Along with us was our newest and most cherished blessing, our four-month-old daughter Brittany. After battling the snow and ice storms that slowed our progress by one full day, we finally pulled into my grandparents' driveway. As we entered the house, the expressions on the faces of my family and the spirit of despair that I discerned all but told what no one wanted to say. Finally, my aunt, choking back tears and reeling under the weight of her own words, said, "He's dying." We entered the room where my grandfather would breathe his last breath, and nothing could have prepared me for the heavy dose of reality that blindsided me. The frailty of this life was staring me in the face with the unblinking truth; natural death is certain. Where is he, I thought? Where is my grandfather? Now a shell of his former self, like a glove without a hand, I saw, first-hand, the quick and devastating effect of cancer, a consequence of the sin curse of Adam, death. After gathering enough strength to open his eyes one last time, my grandfather stared as long as he could as I held the great grandchild that he had never seen in front of him. A tear rolled down his cheek and he closed his eyes, never to open them again. Several hours later, he passed by way of the earth . . . .

As I stood there, I recall thinking that our bodies will return to the dirt of the earth from whence they came. We only live in this tent of flesh temporarily. The Lord then spoke to me, saying, "I do not look on the outward appearance but the heart. Because the body perishes, it does not mean that the soul will if it is given back to Me." What concerns God is the condition of your soul. Is your soul dying? Sin has the same consuming effect on the soul that cancer has on the body. Are you suffering from the spiritual cancer of sin that eats away at the life of your soul? I bring you good news today! There is healing for your sin-sick soul. Do as my grandfather; accept Christ.

Several days later at the family viewing, I recall seeing many rooms with open caskets at the funeral home. Many loved ones of the deceased were paying respect to their beloved. The Holy Spirit spoke to me saying, "This is how the spirit of man looks to God before you accept the life that I breathe into you. And you have I made alive who were dead in trespasses and sins. You were spiritually dead, but I raised you up with Christ Jesus." I pray that you understand the price that was paid that we might have life. Though you go along working, laughing, talking, and joking, you are dead if you don't accept His Gift of Life. You are spiritually in a coffin if you have not experienced the resurrecting power of salvation into your life. Don't lay in the casket! Get up and answer His call. Come and walk in His marvelous light. Walking in His light means being delivered from our propensity to hide from God. We must remember that in times past, we walked according to the course of this world. We must now learn how to walk according to the will and the Word of God. Worldly principles will not manifest Godly blessings. You must change your course. (vs. 2) You must change your nature. (vs. 3) You must become a new creature. Remember that we are only made alive by being raised up with Christ. (vs. 6) Don't forget that Christ must be the underlying foundation in your life. Do you believe that you are alive and raised up with Christ? Do you believe that you are a child of the King? Do you believe that it is God's desire to bless you?

First Things First

It is my desire to take you back to the actual inception of learning, to erase all knowledge the world has taught you regarding being prosperous (fruitful). God tells us that our thoughts are not His thoughts and our ways are not His ways. (Isaiah 55:5) To do this, we must be transformed by the renewing of our minds. (Romans 12:2) We must modify the way we think. We must efface our minds to the manner in which we think to even sanction our minds to think the way the Lord thinks. When we do this, then we become a new person. It can only occur by being born again, not physically but spiritually. When you become a new person, you must then be taught, just like children, how to walk, talk, and do those mandatory encumbrances to function prosperously. Once we begin to allow the Lord to teach us these things, then we become in His likeness. You will then find yourself seeing things the way He does.

Well, if I must be born again to see the Kingdom of Heaven (John 3:3), how does this occur? You must submit your entire being to the Lord. You must accept Him as your Lord and Savior. Again, not just as a prophet or a teacher, but you must confess before all and believe in your heart that God sent His Son as a propitiation for your sins. You must believe that Jesus died for you and that God raised Him from the dead. This is the very key to ever understanding the will of God in your life. I say this because your blessings will be brought forth through the *obedience* that you have to His will.

Turn your direction from seeking possessions to being possessed by Him that owns everything. God doesn't change His Word; we must change the way we view His Word.

John 15:1–5

1: I am the true vine, and my Father is the husbandman. 2: Every [branch] in me that beareth not fruit is taken away: and every branch that beareth fruit, he purgeth it, that it may bring forth more fruit. 3: Now ye are clean through the word which I have spoken unto you. 4: Abide in me, and I in you. As the branch cannot bear fruit of itself, except it abide in the vine; no more can ye, except ye abide in me. 5: I am the vine, ye [are] the branches: He that abideth in me, and I in him, the same bringeth forth much fruit: for without me ye can do nothing.

The Lord is explicit in enlightening us that it is futile to attempt to do anything without Him. The fruit of the Spirit that leads to obedience and prosperity cannot be produced by human nature. These fruits are: love, joy, peace, long-suffering, gentleness, goodness, faith, meekness, and temperance. We can only bear these life-giving fruits. It is the Holy Spirit that produces the fruit. There is no faking it. What is in you will come to the surface, without question within a season. I can hang a sign on a tree indicating that it is an orange tree. I can use every form of advertisement known to man stating my case. However, when an apple comes forth from that tree, no matter what I try to do to persuade you, the reality is that the tree is an apple tree. A tree is known by the fruit that it bears. Are you bearing Godly fruit? If not, the scriptures teach us that if we are not bearing the effervescent fruit that God produces in us, we will be hewn down.

In the book of Matthew, there is a servant that is given one talent by his Lord. He takes the talent and hides it in the earth. Where does man come from? The dust of the earth. This servant took the talent that his Lord gave him and hid it in himself. He hid it in his bank account. He hid it in his household. He took the talent that his Lord gave him to multiply and buried it in his own agenda. We all know that the talent that he was given was taken from him and given to the one that was fruitful with his talent. This "wicked and slothful" servant was cast into outer darkness where there is much weeping and gnashing of teeth. I will say it just like He has given it to me. Don't try to con God. If you are looking to serve the Lord for only what you can get out of it, then you are in it for the wrong purpose. Being blessed is one of His many benefits, not the purpose for serving Him.

Summary Principles

Desire excellence and understand that you must travel the road of excellence.

Pseudo-excellence is the appearance of excellence without the substance.

A taste of real excellence is better than an abundance of pseudo-excellence.

Man can be fooled, but not God or even Satan.

God desires to speak volumes of blessings in your life.

You must first accept Christ in your heart before you receive His blessings.

Put God first. Seek to do His will in your life.

Seek a relationship with the Keeper of your blessing.

It is in the vein of obedience and faithfulness to His will that you will find yourself in the place to allow His blessings to flow.

Include this in your morning devotional time:

Daily Prayer

Nothing can keep me from obtaining God's best.

Nothing can keep me from realizing the vision that God has placed before me.

Nothing can keep me from reaching my maximum excellence in God.

Lord, I will allow You to have Your way in my life. Now help me to rest in You.

I can do all things through Christ which strengthens me.

In Jesus' name.

People that are prosperous in God (fruitful) make a commitment to doing the things that people that are not prosperous won't commit to. Why can't you live where you want? drive what you want? have God's best in your life? God is able to do exceeding and abundantly more than we can ask or think. (Ephesians 3:20) That's amazing. Whatever you can even imagine in terms of being blessed, you still cannot fathom how much more there is. We cannot get the notion wrapped around our finite minds of the possibilities. I say perpetually, don't be angry with those that are enjoying the fullness of His blessings, because you don't know what they had to endure to get in that place to be blessed. Don't make the mistake of seeking the things. It's not the things you acquire but the place you are in God that will bless you.

For as long as my wife and I have been married, not one day has passed that we have not communicated with one another. What kind of a relationship would we have if we didn't talk to each other every day? We live in the same house and are striving for common goals. If I don't speak to my wife, there is something wrong. If we are not communicating, something will get out of sync. And that is what God is saying — "you have to talk to Me. I need to direct you, give you the vision, exhort you, and empower you." God is saying, "I desire a relationship with you." Membership in church is not enough. For it is out of relationship that membership will be established and solidified.

Take Action
Exercise I-1

List the things that hinder you from spending quality devotional time with God. Include those things that keep you from faithfully assembling in the House of God. These things, my friend, are standing between you and experiencing the fullness of God's blessings in your life. The enemy can deceive you into prioritizing all of these things over the Provider of all of these things. But seek ye first the kingdom of God, and his righteousness; and all these things shall be added unto you. (Matthew 6:33)

Take Action
Exercise I-1

"Things" that are keeping me from spending quality devotional time with God.

H I N T S

Working Overtime

☙

Crowded Social Calendar

☙

Excessive Television Time

☙

_____

_____

_____

_____

_____

_____

_____

_____

_____

_____

_____

_____

_____

_____

_____

_____

_____

_____

_____

_____

_____

_____

_____

_____

_____

21

Take Action
Example Exercise I-2
Organizing Devotional Time

On the next page is a sample devotional time outline. Use it as an example to frame **your** commitment to God.

EXAMPLE DEVOTIONAL TIME OUTLINE

	SUNDAY	MONDAY	TUESDAY	WEDNESDAY	THURSDAY	FRIDAY	SATURDAY
5:00 a.m.	Begin Fast			Begin Fast			
5:30 a.m.							
6:00 a.m.							
6:30 a.m.							
7:00 a.m.		Personal Devotion	Personal Devotion	Personal Devotion	Personal Devotion	Personal Devotion	
8:00 a.m.	Personal Devotion						
8:30 a.m.							Personal Devotion
9:00 a.m.							
9:30 a.m.	Begin Church Service						
10:00 a.m.							
10:30 a.m.							
11:00 a.m.							
11:30 a.m.							
12:00 noon							
12:30 p.m.							
1:00 p.m.	End Church Service						
1:30 p.m.	End Fast						

Continued, next page

EXAMPLE DEVOTIONAL TIME OUTLINE

	SUNDAY	MONDAY	TUESDAY	WEDNESDAY	THURSDAY	FRIDAY	SATURDAY
1:30 p.m.	End Fast						
2:00 p.m.							
2:30 p.m.							
3:00 p.m.				End Fast			
3:30 p.m.							
4:00 p.m.							
4:30 p.m.							
5:00 p.m.							
5:30 p.m.							
6:00 p.m.							
6:30 p.m.							
7:00 p.m.							
7:30 p.m.				Begin Church Service		Begin Choir Rehearsal	
8:00 p.m.							
8:30 p.m.							
9:00 p.m.	Family Devotion	Family Devotion	Family Devotion		Family Devotion	End Choir Rehearsal	
9:30 p.m				End Church Service			
10:00 p.m.	Personal Devotion	Personal Devotion	Personal Devotion		Personal Devotion	Personal Devotion	Family Devotion

Take Action
Exercise I-2

Organizing Devotional Time

For manifold blessings to be unleashed in your life, you must prepare yourself for the spiritual forces that will come to hinder them. Spiritual preparation consists of the following:

A Prayer Life – Devotional time with God. Commit to a time each day that you will not allow any person, place, or thing to interrupt you. During this time, read the Word, pray, and meditate. Seek His will for your life daily.

Study Time – God speaks to us through His Word. We must devote time to studying His Word. How can you receive instructions without the instruction manual?

Consecration – Fasting is how we mortify carnality and our will so that we can be spiritually led to do the Lord's. Commit to fasting at least once a week until noon. Soon, you will find yourself fasting until 3:00 p.m. Remember, fasting is not just denying yourself food, it is actually seeking and meditating on God. Food fasts are not the only type of fast. Don't just turn over the plate; seek God. He may have you turn off the television to seek Him.

	SUNDAY	MONDAY	TUESDAY	WEDNESDAY	THURSDAY	FRIDAY	SATURDAY
5:00 a.m.							
5:30 a.m.							
6:00 a.m.							
6:30 a.m.							
7:00 a.m.							
8:00 a.m.							
8:30 a.m.							
9:00 a.m.							
9:30 a.m.							
10:00 a.m.							
10:30 a.m.							
11:00 a.m.							
11:30 a.m.							
12:00 noon							
12:30 p.m.							
1:00 p.m.							
1:30 p.m.							

EXAMPLE PERSONAL DEVOTIONAL TIME OUTLINE

Continued, next page

EXAMPLE PERSONAL DEVOTIONAL TIME OUTLINE

	SUNDAY	MONDAY	TUESDAY	WEDNESDAY	THURSDAY	FRIDAY	SATURDAY
1:30 p.m.							
2:00 p.m.							
2:30 p.m.							
3:00 p.m.							
3:30 p.m.							
4:00 p.m.							
4:30 p.m.							
5:00 p.m.							
5:30 p.m.							
6:00 p.m.							
6:30 p.m.							
7:00 p.m.							
7:30 p.m.							
8:00 p.m.							
8:30 p.m.							
9:00 p.m.							
9:30 p.m							
10:00 p.m.							

Notes

_____
_____
_____
_____
_____
_____
_____
_____
_____
_____
_____
_____
_____
_____
_____
_____
_____
_____
_____
_____
_____
_____
_____
_____

Notes

Chapter Two

Walking In Authority

What is Your Name?

(Mark 5:1–10)
1: And they came over unto the other side of the sea, into the country of the Gad´a-renes. 2: And when he was come out of the ship, immediately there met him out of the tombs a man with an unclean spirit, 3: Who had [his] dwelling among the tombs; and no man could bind him, no, not with chains: 4: Because that he had been often bound with fetters and chains, and the chains had been plucked asunder by him, and the fetters broken in pieces: neither could any [man] tame him. 5: And always, night and day, he was in the mountains, and in the tombs, crying, and cutting himself with stones. 6: But when he saw Jesus afar off, he ran and worshiped him, 7: And

cried with a loud voice, and said, What have I to do with thee, Jesus, [thou] Son of the most high God? I adjure thee by God, that thou torment me not. 8: For he said unto him, Come out of the man, [thou] unclean spirit. 9: And he asked him, **What is thy name?** And he answered, saying, My name [is] Legion: for we are many. 10: And he besought him much that he would not send them away out of the country.

What is your name? That is an awesome question that Jesus asked the man. "Do you know who you are?" the Lord asked the man. The man knew who Jesus was. He called him the Son of the most high God. I will pose this question to you: Do you know who you are? If you don't know who you are, then you will allow Satan and anyone else to tell you who you are. You will allow the past to decree who you are and failures to ordain who you are. You will allow who you once were to bind you in the chains and fetters of the past. Notice that Jesus asked the man his name. Who answered? The unclean spirit did. Do you know who Jesus is and what authority He has given us? Do you understand that your name has been changed? Do you realize that you have the power and authority to no longer run naked through the tombs of this life, crying, and abusing yourself. Once you give your life to Jesus, do you know what God calls you? He calls you His son or daughter. You are loosed from the bondage of being a spiritual orphan. Now walk in the authority that has been given to you. It's time to let the devil know who you are. By doing so, you're letting him know who he is . . . a defeated enemy.

In Mark 5:15, the man is sitting at the feet of Jesus, clothed and in his right mind. He was sitting. He had submitted to Jesus and the Lord was telling this man who he was. The Lord was revealing to this man something that for a long time had eluded him — his name, his identity, and his authority. There is something about knowing who you are in Christ that gives you the boldness not to accept anything less than what you have been given.

Once while boarding a business flight, I could not find my seat. A flight attendant saw my confusion and frustration and came to my aid. After looking at my boarding pass, she politely told me that I had a first-class ticket. I had been in the coach section of the plane at the time because that is what I was accustomed to flying. The company that I worked for purchased only first-class tickets. I had a first-class ticket but a coach-class "mentality." That is what the Lord is trying to get us to understand. He has first-class blessings waiting for us. We must learn to expect excellence in Him while serving Him in excellence as well.

Jesus I know, and Paul I know; but who are ye?
(Acts 19:15)

Walk in God's authority. The enemy doesn't care how much we shout or threaten. What he does recognize is God's Word and God in us. When we walk in authority, it must be according to the will and the Word of God.

(Mark 10:46–52)
46: And they came to Jericho: and as he went out of Jericho with his disciples and a great number of people, blind Bar-ti-me´us, the son of Ti-me´us, sat by the highway side begging. 47: And when he heard that it was Jesus of Nazareth, he began to cry out, and say, Jesus, [thou] son of David, have mercy on me. 48: And many charged him that he should hold his peace: but he cried the more a great deal, [Thou] son of David, have mercy on me. 49: And Jesus stood still, and commanded him to be called. And they call the blind man, saying unto him, Be of good comfort, rise; he calleth thee. 50: And he, casting away his garment, rose, and came to Jesus. 51: And Jesus answered and said unto him, What wilt thou that I should do unto thee? The blind man said

unto him, Lord, that I might receive my sight. 52: And Jesus said unto him, Go thy way; thy faith hath made thee whole. And immediately he received his sight, and followed Jesus in the way.

Take Authority by Taking Action

Stop complaining to God and start calling on Him. Stop fussing and start entrusting. Stop **pro**testing and start **pro**claiming. Complaining demands no performance on our part. If we complain, we are not asking the Lord's assistance. Why, sometimes, do we do this? Many times it is because if we call on God, it will require us to take some form of action in our lives. We, then, must live up to our responsibility. Calling on God to help us in areas that we have infirmities will elicit a response from God that will require action on our part. As you read, you will notice times throughout the course of this book that I will ask you to stop and take immediate action. This is imperative to begin to recreate lasting changes in you life. We must begin with the seemingly simple areas in our lives to begin to transform and renew our minds to conform to the excellence of God's agenda. Bar-ti-me´us took action. He cast away the garment that identified him as a beggar and ran to Jesus. You do the same. Begin to take authority in your life by taking action. What was Bar-ti-me´us asking for? He wasn't asking for a handout. He just wanted his sight so that he could help himself. The fact that he wanted help to help himself is awesome! When Jesus asked him, "What wilt thou that I should do unto thee," He didn't ask for money or to be given favor with some rich man to take him in. Bar-ti-me´us wanted his sight. Stop begging God for a raise on your job. Start asking Him to give you the strength to go to night school so that you can position yourself to demand more. Ask for help to help yourself. **TAKE AUTHORITY** and **TAKE ACTION**! Stop begging God for a new home. Ask for the discipline to get out of debt and the wisdom to manage what you already have so that you can go and get what you want. **TAKE AUTHORITY** and **TAKE ACTION**!

The Holy Spirit Will Empower You to Take Action

There is something about when God delivers you, friend; you are absolutely delivered. When I was young in the Lord, I remember listening to my pastor minster a sermon entitled "The one thing that you don't want to give up is keeping you from going higher in God." I loved the Lord and was excited about my new-found salvation. I wanted a closer walk with Him and marveled at the profound nature of His Word. Life was new and vibrant. I began to see things like I had never seen them before. I also loved drinking beer and other alcoholic beverages. There was a war going on inside of me. It was the old man versus the new man. The new man was getting strong. This spiritual man was alive and growing. The old man wanted to hold onto his carnal ways and dependencies in sin. I came clean with God. I said, "Lord, search my heart and see that I want the more of you." There was a calling on my life and the gift in me was stirred. I asked the Lord to help me stop indulging in happy-hour festivities and beer-bash weekends. I will never forget the profound words that God imparted to me. He said, "Draw nigh unto me and I will draw nigh unto you." From Sunday until Wednesday, I meditated and read the Word. What was I doing? I was casting away my beggar's garment and making my way to Jesus like blind Bar-ti-me´us did. I was calling on the Son of David to have mercy on me. While fasting until noon on Wednesday, I was reading I John 4:4. — Ye are of God, little children, and have overcome them: because greater is he that is in you, than he that is in the world. My God! The Holy Spirit had brought the Word to life for me. Suddenly, a powerful rush of power came upon me, unlike anything that I experienced before. It was the power of the Holy One coming to deliver me — to sweep my temple clean of the desire to drink alcohol. As I stood there alone in the closed office of a corporate tower, God was filling me with the precious gift of the Holy Spirit. He whispered one of the sweetest yet powerful things that I had ever heard. He said, "I have taken the desire of alcohol from you." PRAISE BE TO GOD! He has since shown me the power of deliverance in other areas of my life, as well. Friend, let the power of Almighty God rest upon you. If you are burdened down with dependencies that you cannot get a handle on, let God deliver you. Hear what I am saying. God will dislodge the desire. God will discharge the taste. To liberate you from cigarettes, alcohol, sexual immorality is what Christ came to accomplish. Question: When your car has a defect or needs service, where is the best place to take it? To the manufacturer. Who is our creator? God is. There is nothing that He can't reconstruct, resurrect, or restore. Just come clean with Him. Tell Him, "Lord, I enjoy engaging in these activities and I need You to help me." The most difficult aspect of deliverance is not God having the power. It is us truly wanting to be delivered. Think about that. Amen.

A more excellent way is not just action. It is in the way you see, speak, and hear, as well.

See Through the Lens of Faith
Magnify the Lord

To magnify the Lord is to see Him as He really is. God is almighty. God is all powerful. God is all knowing. God is already bigger than anything that we can imagine with our finite minds. We must, however, begin to see Him as larger than our weaknesses, circumstances, and trials. Commit now to no longer see your dilemma larger than God. See Him through the lens of faith. Several centuries ago, man was limited in what he could see in the universe. Today, with the advent of powerful telescopes, man can see things that he could not see before. Let me ask you, just because man couldn't see it, does that mean that it wasn't there? The same galaxies were there centuries ago; we just needed a more powerful telescope to see them. It is the same way in God. His blessings are there, we just need a stronger lens, or should I say more faith, to see them. Just because you don't see them, it does not mean that they are not there. Why do some seem to be always blessed and others not? Check the strength of their lens (faith).

Faith

During a difficult financial season in our business, I called a meeting and spoke to our employees. I spoke from the heart, saying, "You know the situation that we are in. You can see our condition as a company, financially. I want you all to remember that we don't walk by sight; we walk by faith. We don't look at the external circumstances, but we look at the source of our power.

Many times we heed to the call of God and then begin to work in or within our power to try to make spiritual visions come to pass. God is speaking. God is calling. God will bring it to pass. You must stay in the spiritual place so that He can use you to perform His will. Always remember that His will is not just about you; it is about leading others to learn about Him, as well.

God would not have called us out into the deep waters of faith just to forsake us. The key was to not take our eyes off of God and change our focus to the storms around us. Then God gave me another word. For just as the body without the spirit is dead, so faith without works is dead also. (James 2:26) The Holy Spirit spoke to me. He said, "What do you have around you? Use the resources that I have given you already. You have inventory sitting here collecting dust. Make some things happen; let Me show you what I can do." Believe me, friend, that month of August, when it looked bleak and there were no accounts receivable coming in to meet the accounts payable, we had our most profitable month of that year. All the honor and glory goes to God.

There is Only One Way to the Promises (Promised Land) of God

The Wilderness Experience or "PROCESS"

Deuteronomy 8:2–9
2) And thou shalt remember all the way which the Lord thy God led thee these forty years in the wilderness, to humble thee, [and] to prove thee, to know what [was] in thine heart, whether thou wouldest keep his commandments, or no. 3) And he humbled thee, and suffered thee to hunger, and fed thee with man´-na, which thou knewest not, neither did thy fathers know; that he might make thee know that man doth not live by bread only, but by every [word] that proceedeth out of the mouth of the Lord doth man live. 4) Thy raiment waxed not old upon thee, neither did thy foot swell, these forty years. 5) Thou shalt also consider in thine heart, that, as a man chasteneth his son, [so] the Lord thy God

chasteneth thee. 6) Therefore thou shalt keep the commandments of the Lord thy God, to walk in his ways, and to fear him. 7) For the Lord thy God bringeth thee into a good land, a land of brooks of water, of fountains and depths that spring out of the valleys and hills; 8) A land of wheat, and barley, and vines, and fig trees, and pomegranates; a land of oil olive, and honey; 9) A land wherein thou shalt eat bread without scarceness, thou shalt not lack any [thing] in it; a land whose stones [are] iron, and out of whose hills thou mayest dig brass.

The wilderness experience that we encounter en route to the blessings of God is at many times extremely intense. There are no street signs or traffic lights, only the Word of God to direct us. There is only the faith that has been cultivated, nourished, and persevered in past trials to hold onto. The wilderness will do one of two things: It will exalt you or expose you. The blessings that come through persecution uncover hidden agendas, selfish ambitions, and impure motives. Past hurts will be amplified so that you can address them and be healed. Humility will be learned so that your heart will be lifted up only to God. These processes prepare you to receive God's best in your life. You will be taught that God is your source, because all others will be unattainable.

Once, while in a trial of great intensity, I went to God for a word of revelation as to its severity. The Lord took me to Nehemiah 6:15. This scripture points out that it took, under Nehemiah's leadership, 52 days to complete the building of Jerusalem's wall. This is overwhelming, because this assignment should have taken many months, even years to complete. The Lord then spoke to me saying, **"Daryl, the reason the trial that you are in is so intense is because I am doing a work in you in a matter of days that would ordinarily take years."** Glory be to God! Don't look at the severity of the "process"; look at the accomplishment of God in you and through you. He's molding you more in His image. We do, however, have some influence on how long we stay in the wilderness. Disobedience, murmuring, and rebellion will prolong your stay and possibly cause you to miss the promises of God.

Understand the season that God has you in. The enemy deceives many Christians, because often times they misinterpret this. If you are in a season of testing in the wilderness, don't perform as though you are in a season of harvest. When God is cutting, pulling, building character, and delivering you from the bondage of sin, don't direct your focus toward houses and cars. While you are in a proving season, the Lord is feeding you manna. Manna, means "what is it." The Lord is feeding you what you need on a daily basis to prepare you for your blessings. Don't attempt to harvest manna. The Children of Israel attempted to do that and it spoiled.

Delayed obedience is disobedience during the time of the procrastination. God directed Jonah to go to Nin´-e-veh. He opted to go to Joppa instead. Only after three days in the belly of a big fish did Jonah come into obedience. (Jonah 2:1–10)

Inaccurate obedience is disobedience. When God tells you precisely what to do, any deviation in the slightest is disobedience. (I Samuel 15:1–3) The Lord told Saul, king of Israel, to utterly destroy the people of Am´-a-lek and spare not even the women, children, infants, and animals. Saul spared the king of Am´-a-lek and the best of the sheep and oxen. This proved to be a fatal wedge between Saul and God. To obey is better than sacrifice. (I Samuel 15:22)

You are going to have a "wilderness" process. Remember the word *process*. It is up to you how you handle that experience. The Word of God tells us that every man's work will be tried with fire. (I Corinthians 3:13) If you are going to do what God is calling you to do, you will reach a crossroad and have to decide whether or not you are going to trust and believe God. Again, it is a test. It is not according to how things look; it is according to your faith in God. Faith moves God. When your back is against the wall and you still trust Him, that excites Him. But without faith *it is* impossible to please *him*. (Hebrews 11:6) He wants to be glorified, lifted up, and praised in your hearts in all that you do, not just during the sun-drenched, harvest-filled times but for the thunderstorms and the lean times as well. This demonstrates the faith that He is in control of **every** situation.

The Power of the Tongue

Speak the Word of God to your problem; don't speak the problem.

Death and life are in the power of the tongue: . . . (Proverbs 18:21)

Do you realize that what you speak has a major effect on what will occur in your life? So often, we speak curses into our own lives. I was conversing with a young man that is aspiring to be a successful entrepreneur. He would always say to me that he needed money to get his venture off of the ground. I tried to impress upon him that he did not need an infusion of finance. What he needed was an infusion of faith. By constantly stating, "I need money to be successful," he was setting into motion a self-fulfilling prophecy. Instead, thank God for allowing what you *do* have to be enough to be prosperous. Thank the Lord for the means and favor to do what He called you to do. Calleth those things which be not as though they were. (Romans 4:17)

Do not sow curses with your tongue, but sow blessings. This is especially essential when the enemy uses someone to upset you. Change your thought process to speak blessings to others. That's right, do it even when someone cuts you off on the freeway. Don't speak something negative, just say "Bless them, Lord." When you do this, you will find yourself reaping a harvest of blessings back into your life. I have made it a consistent response when asked by someone how I am doing to give an extremely positive verbal reply. My response is usually that I am **"blessed and with favor."** You must begin to do this, also. If your response is "fine" or "okay," is that all you are? Even if you are in a trial or having a challenging day, does this mean that you are not blessed or that you are out of favor with God? Certainly not. So, confess that you are, constantly.

Shake that poverty spirit. You know the one that says, "I can't." If this spirit infiltrates your spirit, it will run cross moor, throughout every aspect of your life, from faith to finances. Repeat this right now and believe that God is backing you up: *"Spirit of poverty, loose, right now, in the name of Jesus."* Did you repeat it? Say it over and over again until you receive it in your spirit. Listen to me! Don't you let any person, place, or thing hold you from your blessings. I mean nothing and no one. If you decide to stay in relationships that keep a yoke around your neck, that is not God's fault. Over and over again, the Lord confronts us to separate ourselves from the spirit that keeps us in poverty. It might be a job or a family member, even a loved one. Friend, you must war in the spirit to free yourself from those who are clogging the pipes of your blessings. Walk in obedience. Walk in authority. Why do you think that the enemy is fighting you so hard? It's amazing the way the devil will fight you over just a glimpse of God's blessings. The reason he is doing this is because he doesn't even want you to perceive what the Lord has for you. If he can prevent you from even perceiving it, then he won't have to fight you in the area of believing it. If you don't believe, then you will not conceive.

Did You Hear What God Said?

My wife was told at an early age that she could not conceive children. This was an issue that weighed upon her heavily as she came into womanhood. She shared with me this concern. The enemy was trying to get us to not even perceive that we could be blessed in this capacity. We put our petition before the Lord in consecration. After a three-day consecration our first daughter, Brittany, was conceived. What am I saying? You must not allow anything to get in the way of your sight and perception of what God can do. We then went to God in belief that . . . he is, and *that* he is a rewarder of them that diligently seek him. (Hebrews 11:6) After that, our blessing was conceived. Since then, in the same manner our second daughter, Brandi, was conceived.

Listen here! The spiritual insight to this will bless your socks off!

We were told by man that we could not conceive. However, after perceiving and believing, God blessed us with two daughters. There is a significance in Him blessing us with daughters. God was showing us: Not only will your wife conceive children, but that which you conceived will be able to conceive children as well. So not only will you conceive the blessings, I won't stop there. The blessings that I give you will be able to bring forth more blessings in the same way that the devil tried to convince you that you could not conceive. Glory be to God! The devil is fighting you so hard because he knows that once the Lord blesses you that it doesn't stop there. The very blessings that God blesses you with will bring forth more blessings. This is what manifold blessings means. We can count the seeds in the fruit, but God can count the trees in the seed.

Choose Favor Over Finances

If you have divine favor, finances are not a problem. You tell me if this adds up in the course of human logic. You are looking to open a business, yet at the same time you have no investment capital. You have no investors looking to invest capital, but God says "Go out and start a business. Leave corporate America and launch your ship into the deep." The question is not what you don't have but what you do have. You have expertise; you have knowledge, and what is most important, you have favor with God. Let's look back at the natural situation again. At the time that God tells you to start a business, your wife is four-months pregnant and you are looking to buy a house. At the same time, you're in debt with school loans that are outstanding. I am sure it sounds like a crazy situation in which to start a business. I am sure that it reasons that the last thing needed under these circumstances is to get an entrepreneurial unction. Well, that person was me! I am not saying that this is for everyone, but if God calls you out, what are you going to do? Trust God! At that time, I was delinquent on past-due tuition bills. The school financial administrator was very cold in dealing with me. The key though was that I was sincere. The Lord was not looking at my past mistakes before giving my life to Him. He knew my heart. As I stated, I was attempting to start a computer integration and consulting company. One day in prayer, the Lord impressed upon me to offer computer systems to trade for the outstanding balance on my tuition. When I went to the school to speak to the financial administrator, I found that he had been moved to another department, and a young man that I had favor with had replaced him. When we met, I explained to him my intentions and immediately the Spirit of the Lord fell upon his office. I'll never forget his words. He said, "Mr. Tate, it is against our normal policy to trade goods and services for tuition. In addition, I am new in this position. However, I am going to make sure that this comes to pass. I don't know why, but there is something about you that has given you favor." To God be the Glory! Too often we are trying to figure out how God is going to deliver us from circumstances, and we start looking for money. We need favor with God and monetary dilemmas are a non-issue. When you have favor with God, all things will work together for good. Don't look for the glory. He will get the glory while you get the good. *And we know that all things work together for the good to them that love God, to them who are called according to his purpose.* (Romans 8:28)

Blessed is the man that endureth temptation.

Don't Lose Your Favor

I was obedient and founded Micro Integration Center and was blessed with a contract with a large company. They, obviously, had me come up there on contract so expeditiously because they had just terminated the individual that was doing the work for them. The work included a lot of computer servicing. The information services director immediately wanted me to do a physical inventory of what computer components they had, because they didn't know.

When you are discussing computer-related items, you are talking about small components that are worth hundreds, and even thousands, of dollars each. There was at least $40,000 worth of inventory that my client had no idea even existed. I remember an unclean spirit came to tempt me. It said, "Steal! Steal! Steal!" The more I tried to resist in my own strength, the more oppressive the spirit became. The Holy Spirit brought back to my remembrance James 1:12. Blessed *is* the man that endureth temptation: for when he is tried, he shall receive the crown of life. I recited that scripture to myself several times while yielding to the power of the Holy Spirit. When light comes in, darkness must leave. As fast as it had come, the evil spirit was gone. Praise God that the Word of God is quick and powerful and sharper than any two-edge sword.

Let me show you where the blessing was. Later that day, I got a call from a young man stating that his company was in the process of giving away 25 computer systems and if I wanted them to come pick them up. To his company, they were obsolete, but, for me, they were God-sent. I sold them, and that turned out to be the capital that launched our company into the marketplace. "I don't know why I thought of you," he told me. In fact, he was only going to try to reach me one time. I know why he thought of me; God laid me on his heart. It was a test to see if I was going to steal. Satan came to tempt me to steal what was a fraction of the real blessing that God had in store for me. Had I yielded to the temptation and not allowed the Lord to help me in a time of intense temptation, I would have missed out on a huge blessing. Praise God for His strength. The more excellent way to fight the enemy is through being Spirit-filled and through God's Word.

When being attacked with a temptation that is overpowering you, don't yield to it! Right where you are, right now stand on the Word. Submit yourselves therefore to God. Resist the devil, and he will flee from you. (James 4:7) Remember that the scriptures say to submit to God, resist the devil, and the devil will flee. We must first submit to God. It is through our submission to God that He empowers us to resist the enemy. By resisting the devil, we are turning away from what he is using to tempt us, and we are turning to God to help us. By doing this, God will empower you over, and instruct you about, the temptation. Ask the Lord for His help. To experience God's best blessings in your life, you must not allow the enemy to take you off course. Remember, when you are tempted, it is because there is a blessing for you just around the corner!

Seek Opportunity in God

Seek opportunity and not security in God. When God opens a door, make a move through the window of opportunity that you have. We began in a 600-square-foot office. Things were comfortable. The salaries of our small staff were being met. There was a burden, however, in my spirit to take my faith to a higher level. The vision that God had given me was broader than where we were. Soon thereafter He showed us a 4,100-square-foot office suite. Initially, it looked as though we were way over our heads. It seemed like something that we could not afford. The Holy Spirit ministered to me through the scripture, For God hath not given us the spirit of fear; but of power, and of love, and of a sound mind (II Timothy 1:7), as, well as, Where *there is* no vision, the people perish: . . . . (Proverbs 29:18) God dealt with me over a course of several weeks. We took the step of faith and moved. Through consistent seed sowing, prayer, and action, the Lord blessed us to fill the entire office with over $100,000 worth of furniture for less than $1,000. By applying His principles in business, we have more than doubled our staff.

The Application of
A MORE EXCELLENT WAY

But be ye doers of the word, and not hearers only, deceiving your own selves. (James 1:22)

But whoso looketh into the perfect law of liberty, and continueth therein, he being not a forgetful hearer, but a doer of the work, this man shall be blessed in his deed. (James 1:25)

You have to consistently strive to continuously improve areas of your life by being a doer of the Word. If you set the goal to consistently commit to continuous improvement, you will far exceed your most unimaginable goals. Think of everything that you do and weigh it against the backdrop of "is there a more excellent way?" What is God's way? What does His word say? The big picture is too overwhelming and we get discouraged. What we must do is begin to commit to consistent improvement on a minute-by-minute, hour-by-hour, day-by-day basis. You will find that minutes turn to hours, days into weeks, and weeks into months. Just by making small and consistent improvements with application of the Word of God, you will find that the big picture is taking care of itself. You will look up and find that you are quantum leaps beyond where you were before you started applying God's principle in your life.

Here is how we get started. If you will commit and then take action — commit and then take action — **COMMIT AND THEN APPLY!** Get this in your spirit. Make a commitment to improve the areas of your life that you will outline. Do this in a consistent and measurable way. Consistency is the vital commitment in the "process" of creating life-changing behavior. Behavior has direct cause and effect consequences. For example, if you are a tardy person, this behavior affects your life in a dynamic way. I call this a **linear influence**. This influence is when your behavior, in this case — tardiness, has an impact across your entire life. Not only are you late for work, but you're late for church, school, personal and business meetings, as well as for paying bills. There are small, conspicuous, and consistent behavior changes that can bring forth the blessings that our past behavior held hostage. Remember being transformed by the renewing of your mind. **Re**newing means bringing back to its original state. What state is that? The condition that God originally gave to man. God did not intend for man to live beneath his privilege. It is time that we get back what has been taken from us or that which we have surrendered to the enemy. Authentic, life-transforming changes are only accomplished through the Word of God. Counterfeit and inferior motivational practices that eliminate Christ as the foundation are pseudo-excellence.

Take Authority.

Take Action
Exercise II-1

List the area that you will **"Challenge"** to take authority of in your life.

List several scriptures — chapter and verse — that you will refer to and meditate upon to create the desired change in your life. Yes, it will take study, meditation, prayer, and even fasting, in some cases. Remember your Devotional Scheduler? That is what it is for. When you are tempted in the challenged area, immediately go to these scriptures to resist the enemy. Soon they will be committed to your memory; eventually they will be etched in your heart. In the fourth chapter of the Book of Matthew, Jesus resisted Satan by executing the Word. (Matthew 4:1–11) Study these verses of scripture. We must follow His perfect example.

Thy word have I hid in mine heart, that I might not sin against thee. (Psalm 119:11)

State each "Challenge" as a positive statement, not as "I Need" but as "I Will."

Example:

Challenge: I will remain celibate until I marry.

Scripture: Galatians 5:16 – *This* I say then, Walk in the Spirit, and ye shall not fulfill the lust of the flesh.

Scripture: I Corinthians 6:18–20 – Flee fornication. Every sin that a man doeth is without the body; but he that committeth fornication sinneth against his own body. 19) What? know ye not that your body is the temple of the Holy Ghost, *which is* in you, which ye have of God, and ye are not your own? 20) For ye are bought with a price: therefore glorify God in your body, and in your spirit, which are God's.

Challenge: I will control my temper.

Scripture: Proverbs 12:16 – A fool's wrath is presently known: but a prudent *man* covereth shame.

Scripture: Proverbs 14:29 – *He that is* slow to wrath *is* of great understanding: but *he that is* hasty of spirit exalteth folly.

Scripture: Ephesians 4:26 – Be ye angry, and sin not: let not the sun go down upon your wrath:

List the action that you will initiate to begin to take authority in your life.

Spiritually

Naturally

Professionally

Financially

Summary Principles

Realize who you are in God.

The authority that we walk in must be God's authority.

Take authority by taking action.

Let God deliver you.

Check your vision.

If you have favor, you don't need money.

If you have favor, you can always get money.

Watch the trap of the enemy that will abort your blessing.

God gave me a miracle of debt cancellation by allowing me to only pay .60 cents per dollar because I manufactured the computers and traded them with a 40-percent margin of profit. ($5,200)

The school financial administrator also dropped the penalties and interest that were accruing. ($4,000)

Once the debt was cleared, I had a new client.

Our family was blessed with a new home.
. . . With men this is impossible; but with God all things are possible. (Matthew 19:26)

Salvation . . .

During lean times God is teaching us to trust him, reminding us to use what He has given us . . .

In the world's system, the more you use something, the more it becomes depleted. Faith is just the opposite. The more you use faith, the stronger it gets, the better it gets, the more you build it.

True Life . . .

Transformation cannot occur outside the Word of God.

Exercise II-1
What Can I Do In
A MORE EXCELLENT WAY?
It is time to take authority by taking action.

I am committing to strive through the Word of God and the power of the Holy Spirit for continuous improvement in the following areas of my life.

Prayer: *Lord God, in the name of Jesus, strengthen me to commit to the* **Challenge** *that will allow me to make the necessary improvements in my life that will cause me to do things Your way — A More Excellent Way.*

Challenge: _____
_____
_____

Scripture: _____

(Action Taken) _____
_____
_____

Scripture: _____

(Action Taken) _____
_____
_____

What Can I Do In
A MORE EXCELLENT WAY?
It is time to take authority by taking action.
Continued

Scripture: _____

(Action Taken) _____

_____

_____

_____

Challenge: _____

_____

_____

Scripture: _____

(Action Taken) _____

_____

_____

Scripture: _____

(Action Taken _____

_____

_____

Scripture: _____

(Action Taken _____

Challenge: _____

_____

_____

Scripture: _____

(Action Taken) _____

_____

What Can I Do In
A MORE EXCELLENT WAY?
It is time to take authority by taking action.
Continued

Scripture: _____

(Action Taken) _____

_____

_____

_____

Challenge: _____

_____

_____

Scripture: _____

(Action Taken) _____

_____

_____

Scripture: _____

(Action Taken _____

_____

_____

Scripture: _____

(Action Taken _____

Challenge: _____

_____

_____

Scripture: _____

(Action Taken) _____

_____

What Can I Do In
A MORE EXCELLENT WAY?
It is time to take authority by taking action.
Continued

Scripture: _____

(Action Taken) _____

_____

_____

_____

Challenge: _____

_____

_____

Scripture: _____

(Action Taken) _____

_____

_____

Scripture: _____

(Action Taken _____

_____

_____

Scripture: _____

(Action Taken _____

Challenge: _____

_____

_____

Scripture: _____

(Action Taken) _____

_____

What Can I Do In
A MORE EXCELLENT WAY?
It is time to take authority by taking action.
Continued

Scripture: _____

(Action Taken) _____

_____

_____

_____

Challenge: _____

_____

_____

Scripture: _____

(Action Taken) _____

_____

_____

Scripture: _____

(Action Taken _____

_____

_____

Scripture: _____

(Action Taken _____

Challenge: _____

_____

_____

Scripture: _____

(Action Taken) _____

_____

Notes

Chapter Three

Stewardship

We have heard some Christians express that when you endeavor to be a good steward by applying decent and in-order (I Corinthians 9:20) principles in respect to handling and budgeting your resources that you are evading a faith relationship with God — By doing so, you are trying to place your faith in your bank account, thus leaving inconsiderable room for you to exercise the kind of faith that demonstrates miracles in your life. I believe that the opposite is true. Trials will find you at whatever level of stewardship you practice. It is, however, your level of stewardship that will determine the level of the trials or "process" that you will experience: light bill paying stewardship problems, light bill paying trials. Just applying God's Word to your resources in a consistent and biblical manner exemplifies a significant level of faith. In fact, stewardship is a vital principle in the excellence of unleashing God's best in your life.

By applying these principles it frees God's Word to have free course in your life. The faith and discipline associated with these principles allows you to experience Red Sea miracles on another level of faith. He has shown us that He can meet our needs; now let's move on to becoming the lender and not the borrower (Deuteronomy 28:12), the head and not the tail. I am not a "prosperity preacher." I am, however, a prosperity believer. (III John 1:2)

Tithing

Tithing is giving to God ten percent of all of your increase. That is to say your gross income, again, before taxes. God said in His Word (Malachi 3:10), Bring ye all the tithes to the storehouse, that there may be meat in mine house, and prove me now herewith, saith the Lord of hosts.

You must trust that God's way is the more excellent way in this area. You must have the experience for yourself. The enemy fights us tooth and nail in this area because he knows that here lies a major, foundational principle of the covenant to your blessings. Prove me now saith the Lord.

And see that I don't open the window of Heaven and pour you out a blessing that you don't have room enough to receive. We've done it the world's way for so long that sometimes it is difficult to trust God.

Luke 5:1–9

1: And it came to pass, that, as the people pressed upon him to hear the word of God, he stood by the lake of Gen-nes´-a-ret, 2: And saw two ships standing by the lake: but the fishermen were gone out of them, and were washing [their] nets. 3: And he entered into one of the ships, which was Simon's, and prayed him that he would thrust out a little from the land. And he sat down, and taught the people out of the ship. 4: Now when he had left speaking, he said unto Simon, Launch out into he deep, and let down your nets for a draught. 5: And Simon answering said unto him, Master, we have toiled all the night, and have taken nothing: nevertheless at thy word I will let down the net. 6: And when they had this done, they enclosed a great multitude of fishes: and their net brake. 7: And they beckoned unto [their] partners, which were in the other ship, that they should come and help them. And they came, and filled both the ships, so that they began to sink. 8: When Simon Peter saw [it], he fell down at Jesus' knees, saying, Depart from me; for I am a sinful man, O Lord. 9: For he was astonished, and all that were with him, at the draught of the fishes which they had taken:

My God! Talking about blessings that you don't have room enough to receive. So blessed that you NEED to be a blessing to someone else in order to even receive all that He has for you. What was the key to Simon's blessings — OBEDIENCE. Lord, though I've tried every way that I know how. Although I don't understand, "nevertheless" at thy WORD, I will be obedient. Don't try to reason how; just obey the Word of God. Notice that in verse five Simon referred to Jesus as "Master," which means teacher. In verse eight, after that experience of obedience, he called him "Lord." We see the Word of God as more than just good teaching; we must humble ourselves to His Lordship in our life. If someone is your lord, then you are in complete obedience to his will. Who is your lord? Is it Jesus or is it your job, home, car, bank account, or spouse? Whatever you are placing in the stead of your obedience to His will has been placed in a lordship position in your life.

The Word of God says pay tithes. Don't trust yourself to rationalize it as Old Testament or New Testament scripture. The more excellent way is to obey God. How can God trust you with more if He can't trust you with less? If He can't trust you to give $100 when He speaks to your heart, how can He trust you with $1,000 or $10,000. The world has an expression, "I have to see it to believe it." Well, God's, way is just the opposite: You have to believe it before you see it.

Sowing Seeds
Hey, That's God's Money!

It is not my intention to promote an agenda that pushes people to give. I understand that the Lord loves a cheerful giver (II Corinthians 9:7). It is, however, my intention to share with others the power that principled giving has.

I have heard preachers get Christians on such an emotional high during the offering of a church service that everyone's wallet or purse is empty after the offering plate has made its rounds. The question I always ask myself is do we truly understand the principle of the miracle of seed sowing? Do you know why you gave? Do you know the power that your sowing really has? Do you realize that giving is a principle that must be coupled with faith and other Godly principles for you to reap the **maximum** of God's blessing in your life?

The Lord said in Genesis 8:22 that as long as the earth remains that there will be seedtime and harvest. Jesus spoke in Matthew 17:20 that if we have the faith as a grain of mustard seed that we will be able to move mountains. Paul spoke in Galatians 6:7 about sowing and reaping. Jesus spoke the parable of the sower. What is the Lord telling us? Everything starts with a seed that is planted. We must use the seeds that we plant to channel and harness our faith. Sowing seeds gives us the opportunity to, by our actions, set faith into action. I can now **"take action"** against the needs that exist in my life. I can be pro-active and aggressively sow a seed of finance, thus showing God that He is my source. I can literally take action with my faith through my finances.

It is more blessed to give than to receive. Why is that? Giving produces more results than receiving. The Word tells us that giving produces multiplied results. Receiving does not. That is why we want to position ourselves to be a blessing in our giving.

Give in the Spirit of Thanksgiving
God Loves a Cheerful Giver

When you sow seeds, thank God in advance for moving on your behalf. Anticipate His inclination by thanking Him in advance for backing up His word. Don't look at the money that you give as being yours. You must look at the tithes and offering that you give as giving the Lord back a portion of what He has given you. You must understand that you are not giving to man, but to God. Whether you are obedient to this principle or not is between you and God. What happens after you give is between who you gave to and God. The two are mutually exclusive as it relates to YOUR blessings. I am not saying to be totally oblivious to whether or not you are sowing your seeds in good soil. I can only make the assumption that you are where God wants you to be. I do want to make the point, however, that your focus should not be so intolerant in concern to the seeds that it hinders you from sowing what God has told you to. Remember, you are not only sowing a seed of finance, but you are sowing a seed of faith that you will reap manifold. If you are deceived into believing that you are giving to man, flesh is in control. There is no doubt that what the pastor, elders, deacons, and administration of a ministry do with your seed should be for the moving forward of the ministry. However, I will say it again; it has absolutely nothing to do with the blessings of those that give with a pure heart. That's good news! Inspect the fruit of those where you assemble; hold leadership accountable, and keep your **focus** on giving to **God**. He is your source.

"I Can't Afford Not to Give!"
Principle of Exponential Growth

Give, and it shall be given unto you; good measure, pressed down, and shaken together, and running over . . . (Luke 6:38)

God has given me a principle that I have been practicing now for several years, and I want to share it with you. He spoke to me and challenged me to constantly increase my seed sowing so that He could constantly increase my faith and prosperity. Here it is in its simplest format. Every season of harvest in my life, I plan to add a zero to my consistent giving. Two years ago, I consistently gave offerings of dollar amounts that were in the tens (i.e.,10, 20, or 30 dollars). This is excluding tithes. (Tithes are what they are, 10 percent of my gross income). By doing this, I was blessed in increase of finances to begin the next year to give consistently in the hundreds. This year, the Lord is calling me to a higher plateau of faith and finance. Recently He has blessed me with the increase of being able to give seed offerings in the thousands. He gets all the glory. Well, you do the math. What's next? The Lord spoke to me saying, "It's up to you where you stop. If you don't stop, I won't stop, because My Word says I can't." It doesn't take a genius to figure out that if you continue this process to the point that you are giving millions of dollars to His Kingdom, that your needs are taken care of. In fact, you are lending and not borrowing, the head and not the tail, above and not beneath. I'm talking about blessings overtaking you, blessings that will chase you down. With that perspective, I can't afford not to give!

Giving in Dry Seasons

One evening while on my way home, I had car trouble. The cost to repair a broken timing belt and other damage was $725. Our family was on a strict budget to get out of debt. As if He needed to, I reminded God of that reality. He spoke to me (Isaiah 26:3) "Keep your mind focused on Me, and I will keep you in perfect peace." Several days later, I was called to meet with the finance manager at the university that I was attending. When I arrived, he had a computer printout in his hand, which I assumed was a bill for outstanding tuition. Much to my surprise, it was a reimbursement voucher for $950 credit for overpayment of tuition. I remembered on the previous Sunday that I had sowed a special seed offering of $100. God was revealing Himself to me. I cannot afford not to give. I can not afford not to honor God with His money. I can not afford not to trust God.

I just want to encourage those of you doing what you believe the Lord has called you to do, but you're in a storm right now. Keep trusting and believing God, and watch Him move. During our trial or processing season, we cannot stop sowing seeds. To the contrary, take an offensive approach in your sowing. Continue to pay your tithes and give an offering as God leads you. This is a very important aspect of faith. We can say it with words, but God is going to see if we are going to back it up with action. That action is continuing to believe and trust in Him with tithes and offerings, as well as with your time and resources. Then, just as He said to Abraham, He can say to you, now I know. In the presence of your enemies, He will bless you. It is not where you are naturally; it is where you are in Him that matters.

Debt

Speak to the Root of the Problem,
Not the Symptom.

What is keeping us from allowing the Lord to direct our paths to prosperity? One major obstacle is debt. It is the temporary fix that we use to attempt to fill the divine void that only God can fill through obedience to His will for our lives. In many cases, money, or a lack thereof, is only a symptom of the real problem. The underlying issue can be a lack of discipline with your finances. The disciplining and prioritizing of your finances are taking a back seat to the spirit of poverty that is often fueled by impulsive behavior. We then find ourselves in a position of bondage to the lender. This is a device of Satan to keep you oppressed. This also ultimately affects and reflects our integrity. Far too often, the over extension of debt causes us to break covenants and vows that we have entered into.

The borrower is servant to the lender. (Proverbs 22:7) What is hindering us from formulating a plan and believing God?

Bad Debt

Can the Lord trust you with favor? — not just lip service but the kind of trust that is built through growth. Realize that God looks at a person's heart.

The trial was only the practice for the real test. The test of Him keeping you above water during the season of financial tribulation was to prepare you to take action when He restores you. Now you have the experience that He can keep you when your out-go exceeds your income. Surely, He can sustain you while you're on a budget, a budget that will allow you to pull the weeds of bad debt from your life. How do you know that you can maintain a budget? Because He kept you when you had nothing.

Faith in the trial was part one of the test. Part two begins when restoration begins. When you come out of the trial, what are you going to do? Will you conveniently forget the vows that you made before and during the trial. Listen, friend, just because man may write off your bad debt, does not mean that God has. If a creditor reports you as having a charge-off and stops pursing you, it does not necessarily mean debt cancellation. It means that your creditor has decided that pursing you is costing them more than they would recover if you paid them.

True debt cancellation will not affect your good name. The Bible says that a Good name is to be had rather than silver and gold.
(Proverbs 22:12)

What are you doing when you break covenants? In its most simple form, you are lying. You said that you would facilitate your end of the exchange. If you don't, you are a covenant breaker.

These weeds of curses are choking down the good seed that you are sowing.

Whatsoever a man soweth, that shall he also reap. (Galatians 6:7)

What happens when you allow bad debt to go unchecked? You will find that even if you are sowing seeds into the Kingdom, every time that you receive a blessing, a problem crops up and pulls from it. Problems in the form of unexpected bills and breakdowns. What is that? The weeds are coming up!

The wicked borroweth, and payeth not again:
but the righteous showeth mercy, and giveth.
(Psalm 37:21)

Better [is it] that thou shouldest not vow, than
that thou shouldest vow and not pay.
(Ecclesiastes 5:5)

Can God Be Proud of You With What He Has Given You?

We must speak what God says speak. We must speak to the root of the problem. Stop speaking to the external symptoms. We make our mistake by dealing only with what we can see. Let's go deep into the underlying issues. Issues of character and integrity, issues that we need to address. Let me give you an example. When I was in $27,000 of bad debt and desiring to buy a house, that was a symptom of the real problem. Come on now, $27,000 is nothing for God. The real problem was not the money nor God giving me a house. God wanted to deliver me from covenant breaking and undisciplined impulsive spending. The issue was my integrity and character. I could not shout past it, dance over it, or believe only the scriptures that I wanted to believe to get by it. He took my desire and vision and used it to make me more like Him.

What is the more excellent way to handle bad debt? Honor your vow. What if the company charged it off? Honor your vow. What if they've stopped harassing you about it? Honor your vow. Do you get the picture? Being a good steward and actually applying God's principles to your finance actually takes more faith in Him than just naming and claiming or blowing things off. You must trust God to keep you while you work out the mess that you've made, while He works out the mess in you. All the while you are cleaning up what you've messed up, He's building your character, building your faith in Him to keep you during that time. He's disciplining you so that when you do come out, you will stay out. Too many Christians subscribe to the "microwave," instant teaching about faith in God. Let's understand that God is a decent and in-order God. (I Corinthians 14:40) Why would He bless you with a house if you don't have the discipline to pay your bills in an apartment? Why would He set you up to fail like that? Be faithful in a few things and watch Him make you a ruler over many. Again, I'm not talking about the Lord meeting your needs. His Word says that He shall supply all of our needs according to His riches in glory. (Philippians 4:19). I'm speaking of unleashing the blessing of lending and not borrowing; the head and not the tail, above and not beneath.

Not one of us is exempt from storms and trials in our lives. Some trials shake our foundation and we find ourselves devastated in the mist of bad debt and bad credit. We kept the faith throughout the trial and trusted God until it blew over. We sometimes forget that how we react after the trial is just as important as how we stood in it. God is saying, "Don't stop trusting Me now. Trust Me to restore your good name as well. I want to make you whole in that area as well." Let me illustrate it this way; Take a hurricane for example, once the winds have ceased and the rain has stopped, we find ourselves standing, if we built our house on a solid foundation. (Matthew 7:24) Once the storm is over, our house stands, but some cleanup is in order. Perhaps some windows have been shattered, roof shingles destroyed, even the garden uprooted. It is the same with trials that affect our finances. We stood fast in the trial, now the second test is what we will do afterward. Will you let things lay in waste around you or continue to believe God will make you whole? That is, better than you were before the trial. The storm was part one of your process. He kept you when you were going without. Now you know that He can keep you while you are on a budget, paying back vows that you made.

Budget

If your out-go exceeds your income, your upkeep is your downfall.

Balance your budget! If you must, reduce your expenses. Take a good look at eliminating unneeded out-go. For example, maybe your entertainment expenses are too high. Perhaps you will need to eliminate your eating out or cable channels for a season or two. Some budget balancing may require that you sell one of your vehicles or trade for a lesser car note. Moving to a home or apartment that has a lower monthly payment may be necessary. Be sure that your budget is balanced to accommodate the necessary allocation for savings and debt reduction.

Monthly Budget
A More Excellent Way Budget Plan

Total Monthly Net Income _____

Your total monthly income minus your total monthly expenses is the amount of money that you have available to allocate for savings and debt reduction.

Monthly Out-go	Funds Allocated	Desired Allocation
Tithes & Offerings		
Rent/Mortgage		
Repairs		
Utilities		
Water		
Lights		
Gas		
Telephone		
Car Expenses		
Notes		
Gasoline		
Maintenance		
Other		
Food		
Entertainment		
Cable TV/Movies		
Eating Out		
Other		
Clothing		
Credit Cards		
Loans		
Insurance		
Life		
Auto		
Other		
Tuition		
Dry Cleaning		
Other Expenses		
Savings		
Debt Reduction		

Pulling Weeds
Bad Debt Reduction

Enter into new covenant agreements with bad debt creditors in writing. Bad debt is debt that is delinquent or has been charged off. Allocate funds from the debt reduction portion of your budget to honor your new covenant. If interest is a factor, pay off the balances accumulating the highest interest first. When interest is no longer a factor, allocate the largest portion of your budgets debt reduction fund to the oldest bills. Once these bad debts are under new covenants and being paid off, make sure that your new payment history and payoff is being reported to the proper credit reporting agency in your area.

Pulling Weeds
Bad Debt Reduction Worksheet

Debt	Total Balance Owed	Monthly Payment	Interest Rate	Date Paid Off

Once You Have Paid Off All Bad Debt, Begin to Attack Your Existing Debt

Debt	Total Balance Owed	Monthly Payment	Interest Rate
Visa	$ 240.00	$ 20.00	16.00%
Auto Loan	$ 5,000.00	$ 300.00	11.00%
Student Loan	$ 3,500.00	$ 200.00	5.00%
Consolidation Loan	$ 2,100.00	$ 65.00	10.00%
MasterCard	$ 100.00	$ 20.00	17.00%
Home Mortgage	$72,000.00	$ 700.00	8.00%
Department Store	$ 420.00	$ 30.00	19.00%

Assume that you have allocated $100.00 per month in your budget for debt reduction.

In what order would you attack this debt?

First, let's start with the MasterCard, because it can be paid off the fastest. This loan also has the highest interest rate. Once it is paid off you will have an additional $20.00 per month to allocate for debt reduction in your budget.

The Visa card is the next appropriate note to pay off. Be sure to apply the additional funds that you have from paying off the MasterCard. Again you are attacking the next lowest pay-off balance. Another incentive is the 16 percent interest rate that is being paid.

The department store charge card is the next lowest balance owed with a high interest rate. After paying off this debt, you should have $70.00 more per month available for debt reduction. (MasterCard – $20.00, Visa – $20.00, and the department store credit card – $30.00)

Next attack the consolidation loan. We are still following the route of paying off the next lowest balance. Once this debt is paid off add another $65.00 per month for debt reduction ($135.00). The next lowest debt is the student loan; however let's look at the big picture. We are paying a much higher interest rate on our car loan. In addition, if we pay the car off, we will decrease our insurance payment, thus leaving more for savings and debt reduction.

The student loan is the final payoff before we attack our home mortgage. Notice that once out of debt that there is $635.00 per month available to pay off your home. By adding a principle only payment that matches your existing mortgage payment you will save over $80,000.00 in interest. You will also pay your home off in less than eight years. See home mortgage amortization schedule on page 73.

Attack Your Debt

ount Available for Debt Reduction _____

Debt	Total Balance Owed	Monthly Payment	Interest Rate	Priority of Payoff

HOME MORTGAGE AMORTIZATION SCHEDULE

APR	Purchase Price	Additional Monthly Principle Payment	Finance Charges	Total Paid	Monthly Note	Total Number of Payments
8.00%	$50,000.00		$82,079.92	$132,079.92	$366.88	360 — 30 Years
8.00%	$50,000.00	1/2 of Monthly Note $183.44	$27,080.31	$77,080.31	$366.88	141 — 11.75 Years
8.00%	$50,000.00	Monthly Note $366.88	$16,882.66	$66,882.66	$366.88	92 — 7.6 years
APR	Purchase Price	Additional Monthly Principle Payment	Finance Charge	Total Paid	Monthly Note	Total Number of Payments
8.00%	$100,000.00		$164,160.47	$264,160.47	$733.76	360 — 30 years
8.00%	$100,000.00	1/2 Monthly Note $366.88	$54,160.76	$154,160.76	$733.76	141 — 11.75 years
8.00%	$100,000.00	Monthly Note $733.76	$33,765.39	$133,765.39	$733.76	92 — 7.6 years
APR	Purchase Price	Additional Monthly Principle Payment	Finance Charges	Total Paid	Monthly Note	Total Number of Payments
8.00%	$150,000.00		$246,229.76	$396,229.76	$1,100.65	360 — 30 years
8.00%	$150,000.00	1/2 Monthly Note $550.33	$81,240.40	$231,240.14	$1,100.65	141 — 11.75 years
8.00%	$150,000.00	Monthly Note $1,100.65	$50,647.34	$200,647.34	$1,100.65	92 — 7.6 years
APR	Purchase Price	Additional Monthly Principle Payment	Finance Charges	Total Paid	Monthly Note	Total Number of Payments
8.00%	$200,000.00		$328,309.52	$528,309.52	$1,467.53	360 — 30 years
8.00%	$200,000.00	1/2 Monthly Note $733.76	$108,320.55	$308,320.55	$1,467.53	141 — 11.75 years
8.00%	$200,000.00	Monthly Note $1,467.53	$50,647.34	$267,530.06	$1,467.53	92 — 7.6 years

Investing

Once you have eliminated your debt, investing is a consideration. Ecclesiastes 11:2 – Give a portion to seven, and also to eight; for thou knowest not what evil shall be upon the earth. For the believer, ask yourself these questions. Have I sought God to give Him all that He has given me to give? There is no better investment return than that which God gives to us for supporting Kingdom's work. Secondly, have you met the needs of your family? The Word lets us know that if any man does not provide for his own then he is an infidel and has denied the faith. (I Timothy 5:8)

Thirdly, why am I investing? Am I investing to help further the work of the Lord and to help others in need? These are tough questions that God already knows the answers to. Remember, you cannot fool God.

Understand what you are investing in. God will not bless your investment into immoral ventures.

When does investing become hoarding? Am I just building more barns? A good way to determine your investment strategy is to seek a plan that allows you to live a comfortable, modest, debt-free lifestyle on the dividends of your investment, without having to withdraw from the principle. By doing this, you are being wise like the ant in Proverbs (vs. 6:6). The ant knows that it has a certain season to store up for "retirement." Without any supervision, the ant is diligent in its preparation for seasons that it is unable to work, while at the same time leaving an inheritance for its offspring.

Let's look at the power of investing. No amount is too small. See the investment deposit schedules on the next two pages.

Investment Deposit Schedule

Opening Savings Balance **$100.00**
Annual Rate of Return **12.00%**
Number of Years **10**
Contribution Each Month **$100.00**
Ending Balance **$23,563.94**

Years	Contribution/Yr.	Total
0	$0.00	$100.00
1	$1,200.00	$1,393.61
2	$1,200.00	$2,851.29
3	$1,200.00	$4,494.84
4	$1,200.00	$6,344.70
5	$1,200.00	$8,430.30
6	$1,200.00	$10,780.41
7	$1,200.00	$13,428.57
8	$1,200.00	$16,412.58
9	$1,200.00	$19,775.04
10	$1,200.00	$23,563.94

YEARLY DIVIDEND **$4,171.62**

Opening Savings Balance **$100.00**
Annual Rate of Return **12.00%**
Number of Years **10**
Contribution Each Month **$500.00**
Ending Balance **$161,545.14**

Years	Contribution/Yr.	Total
0	$0.00	$100.00
1	$6,000.00	$6,517.34
2	$6,000.00	$13,748.57
3	$6,000.00	$21,896.90
4	$6,000.00	$31,078.64
5	$6,000.00	$41,424.85
6	$6,000.00	$53,083.22
7	$6,000.00	$66,220.17
8	$6,000.00	$81,023.21
9	$6,000.00	$97,703.64
10	$6,000.00	$116,499.75

YEARLY DIVIDEND **$21,179.73**

Investment Deposit Schedule

Opening Savings Balance **$1,000.00**
Annual Rate of Return **12.00%**
Number of Years **10**
Contribution Each Month **$1,000.00**
Ending Balance **$235,639.46**

Years	Contribution/Yr.	Total
0	$0.00	$1,000.00
1	$12,000.00	$13,936.15
2	$12,000.00	$28,512.93
3	$12,000.00	$44,938.42
4	$12,000.00	$63,447.06
5	$12,000.00	$84,303.06
6	$12,000.00	$107,804.13
7	$12,000.00	$134,285.72
8	$12,000.00	$164,125.84
9	$12,000.00	$197,750.43
10	$12,000.00	$235,639.46

YEARLY DIVIDEND **$41,716.22**

Opening Savings Balance **$1,000.00**
Annual Rate of Return **12.00%**
Number of Years **10**
Contribution Each Month **$2,000.00**
Ending Balance **$467,978.54**

Years	Contribution/Yr.	Total
0	$0.00	$2,000.00
1	$24,000.00	$26,745.48
2	$24,000.00	$55,756.13
3	$24,000.00	$88,446.06
4	$24,000.00	$125,281.89
5	$24,000.00	$166,789.43
6	$24,000.00	$213,561.16
7	$24,000.00	$266,264.72
8	$24,000.00	$325,652.40
9	$24,000.00	$392,571.94
10	$24,000.00	$467,978.54

YEARLY DIVIDEND **$83,037.42**

Summary Principles

God uses the desire that He has given you to mold you into His image.

When I first gave my life to the Lord, I quickly submitted to His principles of tithing and giving an offering. Immediately I was blessed through His Word. Soon after, the Lord challenged me to own up to over $27,000 of delinquent school loans and delinquent consumer debt. He spoke to me clearly and said that the debts were weeds choking down the good seed that I was sowing. Sure I was being blessed, but, remember, whatsoever a man soweth, that shall he also reap. I was ready to be overtaken with blessings not with reaping bad vows.

Many creditors will work with you in relieving bad debt and delinquent outstanding balances. Contact each of them to work out a payment schedule that will fit into your BUDGET. By doing this you are:

Beginning to uproot the weeds that can choke down the harvest of blessings in your life.

Creating a new covenant with your creditors, thus voiding the previous agreement that cursed you as a covenant breaker.

Allowing God to deal with the underlying issues in your character that caused you to be in the situation in the first place.

Trusting Him according to the principles of His Word (faith).

Glorifying God with His money through your actions, therefore, being a powerful witness.

The Lord must see us exercising good stewardship with what He has given us if we expect to receive more.

Stop giving Satan so much credit for lack of preparation and organization (stewardship).

Notes

Notes

Chapter Four

Let God . . .

Healed From Our Past

John 5:1–9
1: After this there was a feast of the Jews; and Jesus went up to Jerusalem. 2: Now there is at Jerusalem by the sheep [market] a pool, which is called in the Hebrew tongue Beth-es´-da, having five porches. 3: In these lay a great multitude of impotent folk, of blind, halt, withered, waiting for the moving of the water. 4: For an angel went down at a certain season into the pool, and troubled the water: whosoever then first after the troubling of the water stepped in was made whole of whatsoever disease he had. 5: And a certain man was there, which had an infirmity thirty and eight years. 6: When Jesus saw him lie, and knew that he had been now a

long time [in that case], he saith unto him, Wilt thou be made whole? 7: The impotent man answered him, Sir, I have no man, when the water is troubled, to put me into the pool: but while I am coming, another steppeth down before me. 8: Jesus saith unto him, Rise, take up thy bed, and walk. 9: And immediately the man was made whole, and took up his bed, and walked: and on the same day was the sabbath.

Come now and let's deal with this. Let's confront the issues in our lives. Do you want to be made whole? Do you want to be blessed? Do you want to be delivered from whatever infirmity is causing you to miss out on God's most choice blessings? Do you want to stand on your own two feet? At the pool at Bethesda there were many people that suffered from various infirmities. These afflictions rendered them impotent, powerless, and incapacitated. The scripture states that these people were waiting for the moving of the water. They were waiting for God to move. They were waiting for an angel to come down and stir the water. What was Christ letting us know when he affronted this man? He IS the living water. He is the resurrection power to raise us up from any circumstance or dilemma. Note that when Jesus asked the man, "Wilt thou be made whole?" the man did not answer the Lord's question. He began to make excuses as to why he was not whole. His inaugural reaction was to figure out how he would be made whole. The impotent man was defeated because he was waiting for man to help him. God is your source. Always remember that. The Lord of lords does not need our excuses, nor does He need us to help Him figure out how we will be made whole. What He wants is an answer to His question. The Lord is asking you, today, "Do you want to be made whole?" Regardless of your past scars, He can heal you. Regardless of your past failures, He can restore you. Regardless of your past weakness, He can empower you. Say yes, right now!

This impotent man had been in that state for so long that he had become compliant to governing factors around him. He had been incarcerated for so long within his infirmity that he had resigned himself to stay in that state. Don't you dare settle for one ounce less than what God has for you. "Rise, take up thy bed, and walk," the Lord said. And immediately the man took up his bed and walked . . . immediately, not later . . . at once, not after a while! Though he was in that state for a long time, he obtained immediate power! Well, what are YOU waiting for? We often say that we are waiting on God, when God is waiting on us. Have you been in "that state" for a long time? Jesus knew about the impotent man and was moved with compassion. And He cares about you with the same clemency.

Release the baggage of your past that is hindering your now blessings. Be healed from the hurt that someone caused you three relationships ago that is causing you to be dysfunctional in your marriage. Lose the baggage that is keeping you from being blessed with a spouse. Be delivered from the bad habits that had you in bondage in the world. In the Name of Jesus, let the Lord resurrect you from the shame that you feel from being abused or molested as a child. If we don't get healed from our past, we will never rise up and walk in the authority given to us. Remember, He wants us to prosper and be in HEALTH as our soul prospers. Health is not restricted to a physical condition. It relates to spiritual, psychological, mental, and emotional conditions, as well. The enemy operates in our past to condemn us. Maybe while in sin you had an abortion. You must be healed from that. Perhaps you were not there for your children. It could have been sexual immorality that held you hostage and now the guilt is weighing you down. The Word of God tells us that if any man *be* in Christ, *he is* a new creature, old things are past away, behold all things are become new. (II Corinthians 5:17)

How Am I Made Whole?

Luke 17:12–19
12: And as he entered into a certain village, there met him ten men that were lepers, which stood afar off: 13: And they lifted up [their] voices, and said, Jesus, Master, have mercy on us. 14: And when he saw [them], he said unto them, Go show yourselves unto the priests. And it came to pass, that, as they went, they were cleansed. 15: And one of them, when he saw that he was healed, turned back, and with a loud voice glorified God, 16: And fell down on [his] face at his feet, giving him thanks: and he was a Sa-mar´i-tan. 17: And Jesus answering said, Were there not ten cleansed? but where [are] the nine? 18: There are not found that returned to give glory to God, save this stranger. 19: And he said unto him, Arise, go thy way: thy faith hath made thee whole.

Notice that these lepers lifted up their voices and cried out to the Lord for mercy. We must humble ourselves before God and admit that we need His divine deliverance in our lives. Is it smoking cigarettes, consuming alcohol, lust for sexual immorality? It could be lying, cheating, or stealing. Perhaps it is a bad temper or gossiping. Perhaps it is that you have poor self-esteem or are prone to enter into abusive relationships. Get the picture? There is a constant need for deliverance and healing in our lives. I want you to notice, however, that although ten were cleansed, only one was made whole . . . the one that glorified God with thanksgiving. The one that was so grateful for the mercy of God that he gave his entire life to him. The other nine were cleansed. They were healed of the disease, thus preventing more damage in the area of their affliction, but only one was completely restored to a state better than before he was inflicted with the infirmity. He was made whole. The leper's faith in Christ had made him whole. The Lord wants to completely restore you and your life circumstances to better than they were before you came to Him. You must glorify Him with thanksgiving . . . not just lip service, but with your life. I see so many people call on the Lord when they are in a great need, only to turn their backs on Him when the pressure has been relieved. That is not giving thanks. That is not having faith in Him.

Speak to Us in the Present

Joshua, Chapter 3 – A more excellent way in God is to be sure to be in that place where God wants you to be. Be sure to hasten to be where God is leading. Joshua told the children of Israel to immediately come when they saw the Ark of the Covenant. (Joshua 3:3) When God was moving, the key was to be in **that** place to be led by God. He told them at the same time not to get too close but to remain in a place where they could see God and where He was moving. What Joshua was letting the children of Israel know and what God is letting us know is that we must hasten to the movement of God, yet at the same time, we must not get ahead of what He wants us to do. We must not get ahead of God.

Sometimes God places in our spirit an ultimate call for our lives. He may reveal to us where we will eventually be. Be careful not to rush ahead of God to get there. Let Him make you by preparing you in the present season of your life.

It is easy for those that are gifted, talented, or educated to have a self-driven will when it comes to purpose. Determination and drive are good, but they are more excellent when in His will for our lives.

There is a way that seemeth right to a man, but the ways therein are death. Leaning to your own understanding can cause death to the ultimate purpose for your life.

My relationship with God was revolutionized

when I truly began to understand the Person of God the Holy Spirit and when I realized His purpose and desire in my life. The wonderful Holy Spirit was calling me to a deeper fellowship and closer communion with Him. He was letting me know that He was more than what I was allowing Him to be, not only the power used by God to deliver me from the bondage of sin. He is God. An important and equal part of the Trinity. Realize that the Holy Spirit has a personality. He can be grieved, and He has a will. The important thing to remember is that the will of the Holy Spirit is always coincident with the Father and the Son. He will point you to the will of the Father and the grace of the Son.

The Holy Spirit will lead you in worship, praise, direction in all truths, whether it is ministry, business, or personal stewardship.

Worship, worship, worship God. God wants to be worshiped. It is important not to provoke to worship but lead in worship. We must learn to yield to the power of the Holy Spirit and not force in praise and worship. I had an experience with the Holy One that I will never forget. I was in my prayer closet praising Him. I was led by the Spirit to look in the mirror. I watched my face intently while in praise as I saw my countenance began to change. It was me in outline form, but my gestures and characteristics were unlike anything that I had ever seen myself do. Suddenly, I began to shout truths from God's Word. Although I was speaking English, my dialect was different. The power of God was resting upon me. This manifestation of God went on for several hours. The Spirit was not overpowering, but He was empowering. Had I backed away at any time, I felt He would have withdrawn. In fact, after several hours the Holy Spirit said to me, "That's enough. I do not want to overwhelm you." He then withdrew. WOW! All I did was ask Him to fellowship with me, to be my companion, to teach me how not to grieve Him, to take me closer to the Father and the Son.

After several of these encounters, I asked the Holy Spirit to show me the more of Him. As I was in praise, He said these words to me, "The only way that I can show you the more of Me is to show you yourself without Me. The only way you can really realize who I am is to see yourself as who you are without Me." "My God! Show me You," I exclaimed! "Whatever it takes." For just an instant, as I looked in the mirror, I could see what looked like a veil of red slide down before my eyes. What it revealed was a sight that was more repulsive than any word that I could ever find to describe it. I have never seen anything like that in my entire life and don't ever want to again. In just a glimpse, I was mortified to the point of breathlessness. I tell you it was indescribable and indefinable. All I could do was fall to my knees with tears running down my face praising Him for His mercy, for the Holy Spirit had allowed me to see, just for a second, mankind in the eyes of God, without the covering of the Blood of Jesus.

Friend, an indwelling and fellowship with the Holy Spirit is the more excellent way in revealing the will of God in your life. To understand and **OBEY** God's will for your life is fundamental in unleashing His blessings. For if you be willing and obedient, you will eat the good of the land. (Isaiah 1:19)

Prepare Us For the Future
Don't Be Scared — Get Prepared

There were servants in the book of Matthew that were given talents by their lord. One had one talent, another two, and the third five. The servant with the one talent did not multiply what was given to him. God called him a wicked and slothful servant. His excuse was that his lord was hard and he was afraid that he might lose what was given to him. Many times we are too afraid to be blessed in God. Fear is a device of deception used by Satan to oppress. Fear is the result of a lack of faith in God. For God has not given us the spirit of fear, but of power and of love and of a sound mind. You can rest assured that if fear is gripping you concerning acting on God's will in your life, it did not come from the Lord. Fear is paralyzing. It will incarcerate you more effectively than a high-security prison. Its results are devastating to achieving excellence in God.

When asking the Lord for courage in times of fear, we all too often make the mistake of looking for an emotion of feeling brave. Feeling brave and being courageous are two different things. Courage is manifested in the times that you may be afraid, but you obey God anyway. When the Lord speaks a word in your life and you decide to walk in authority, it would be naive to think that dark forces will not come to discourage you from doing so. God had been sending prophetic words in my life during a season of preparation through anointed men and women. Some were prophesies; others were confirmations on things that the Lord was dealing with me about. One night while in meditation, I felt the oncoming presence of a foul spirit. This was no imp or small demon. Normally I can rebuke such spirits by merely thinking the Word of God. Again, this was different. As I laid on the floor with my eyes closed, I could feel the massive size and power of this spiritual wickedness. Its width was a horizon, and its height was oppressive. The words it spoke told me that I was on course with God. "You don't want to obey Him," it gutted out. After a short pause, it bellowed, "because if you do, then you will have to deal with me every day." I quickly got up and began to praise God and read the Word. The principality withdrew, but not in a fleeing fashion. The Holy Spirit revealed to me that the principality was a dominion over other spirits — Death, Depression, and Despair. "The reason it was even allowed to visit you was because God is about to usher you to a higher level in Him. It was not to scare you, but to prepare you for upcoming spiritual battles." Much like a flu shot, the dead virus of the flu is exposed to your system. Its purpose is not afflict you, but to allow your immune system to get prepared for when the real virus attempts to infiltrate. This was a spiritual immunization.

Beware of Spiritual Assassins

Genesis 4:1–8
1: And Adam knew Eve his wife; and she conceived, and bare Cain, and said, I have gotten a man from the LORD. 2: And she again bare his brother Abel. And Abel was a keeper of the sheep, but Cain was a tiller of the ground. 3: And in process of time it came to pass, that Cain brought of the fruit of the ground an offering unto the LORD. 4: And Abel, he also brought of the firstlings of his flock and of the fat thereof. And the LORD had respect unto Abel and to his offering: 5: But unto Cain and to his offering he had not respect. And Cain was very wroth, and his countenance fell. 6: And the LORD said unto Cain, Why art thou wroth? and why is thy countenance fallen? 7: If thou doest well, shalt thou not be accepted? and if thou doest not well, sin lieth at the door. And unto thee [shall be] his desire, and thou shalt rule over him. 8: And Cain talked with Abel his brother: and it came to pass, when they were in the field, that Cain rose up against Abel his brother, and slew him.

There are consequences associated with not achieving excellence in God. You will see others making great strides in the Lord, and at first you might even admire them. You will feel the anointing that He has placed upon them. You will see the favor and marvel at the gifts that glorify Him. If you don't seek His excellence in your life, making acceptable sacrifices, you leave space for envy. Admiration turns to envy because you see how the Lord is using them, and want the same blessings. Envy then escalates into jealousy when they are used of God. I've seen it happen this way time and time again. When those that are seeking God's best start to be blessed, those that do not have His blessings begin to spiritually attack and tear them down. It is amazing that people think that holding someone else back is going to move them forward. You must stop the backbiting. You must stop the gossiping and start praying and seeking God's face for His purpose for your life.

Let God Turn Satan's Torment into Testimony

Let me tell you something. No one, I mean no one, can stop the blessings that God wants to bestow upon you . . . well almost no one. Only you can stop them. Satan can use people to hinder but not stop them. Not even other Christians can stop God from blessing you! It was when I learned to take a curse and give back a blessing that I began to really understand the power of the cross.

The television production company that I cofounded was contracted to produce a large multi-day conference. Just before the conference was to begin, the enemy began to fight tooth and nail to destroy our blessing. There was a miscommunication in the negotiated production cost due to substantial requested additions made by the hosting ministry. Immediately our client began to close ranks and terminate the imperative lines of communication, as well as search for others to fulfill production work already agreed upon. All we could do was hang in there until God moved on our behalf. We could not defend ourselves or come to an understanding with our client. We held our integrity and delivered what had been agreed upon by people both far and near the best quality of production and capturing of God's anointing in the history of the conference. We held our peace and let the Lord fight our battles. In fact, a large Christian television network found out about how we kept our integrity and approached us about providing a service for them that now allows us to make exponentially more and provides greater exposure than we could ever have imaged. It does not matter what title, position, or office, man does not hold your blessing.

While we are on our cross, Satan is there mocking just like those that mocked Jesus, saying, "If you are a Christian, come down." He is telling you the easy way. Though the painful and public death is humiliating, it is still the more excellent way. What am I saying? If you must sell one of your cars to get out debt, DO IT. If you must sell your existing home and move into a smaller one with less mortgage and overhead, DO IT. Yes, people may mock you and say that you are going backward, but you know that you are decreasing to later increase. Much like Christ, you are "dying" now so that you can get up in a short time with the power. This is an area that you must ask for God's help. If Jesus had to do it, don't think that you won't. "But, Lord, why do I have to endure this with everyone watching?" Our Savior died a public death so that when He rose there would be no mistake about whether God had really raised Him from the **dead.**

Resurrection Power for your circumstance comes only with the cross.

Jesus got up with all power and then went to Satan's territory and defeated him. He didn't have to fight, he just said, "give Me the keys," and that was it. Are you fighting or are you operating in authority? The authority is the more excellent way. It's like, "Do you know who I am?" and "Do you know who is in Me?"

Prophecies can go forward. People may come up to you and speak a word in your life. You still must bring the vision to pass. You can't just sit on it. You must come into obedience; complete obedience is in yielding to God in those areas that you have not done so. He demonstrates in different areas of our lives; when we yield to Him, it comes out excellent. It is just those areas that we are disobedient, delayed obedient, or afraid that it does not.

If God is blessing over on Main Street, then why am I on Elm Street? That is what we need to ask ourselves.

Come out of always being need-centered. I say this because whatsoever a man soweth that shall he also reap. (Galatians 6:7) If you are constantly sowing need, then you will reap it back multiplied. Stop causing your needs to increase. Understand that God is your source, and He has a superfluous supply that He wants to bestow on you. But my God shall supply all your need according to his riches in glory by Christ Jesus. (Philippians 4:19) Now put your name in this scripture. I'll show you how I recite this scripture. "But Daryl's God shall supply all of Daryl's needs according to His riches in glory by Christ Jesus." Understand, however, that helping someone else in need will invoke the reaping of your needs being met.

Now unto him that is able to do exceeding abundantly above all that we ask or think, according to the power that worketh in us, ... (Ephesians 3:20) Take the limits off of God. One night at four in the morning, the Lord woke me up. He reproved me for not believing Him enough. My wife and I were looking to purchase a new home to accommodate our growing family. We were expecting our second daughter, Brandi, and we needed more room. In our search, we found a house that we both liked and began the pre-qualifying phase for purchase. It was then that the Lord woke me up. He said to me, "Is that all you want? Is that all you expect from me? Daryl, I am disappointed in you. I am a much bigger God than that. Stop believing Me for only things that you can picture in your finite mind. I will bless you with a better house that you will pay much less for! I will bless you to pay for it with cash! Why pay interest? I am a BIG GOD." I immediately woke my wife up right then at four in the morning, and we both repented for setting limits on God. For the next few weeks, we kept ourselves open to hear God. One morning while praying, I asked the

Lord to show me the area that we should look to move. That very morning, He did. There was lakefront property about five miles from us. As I drove through the area, the homes on the rolling-hilled landscaped golf course and lake-view property seemed totally out of our financial reach, from a natural standpoint. I continued on anyway. After meeting with a salesman, we found out that he had a beautiful, affordable lot off of the golf course that had been discounted. We could afford the down payment and began to aggressively pay off the balance. In the interim, the land nearly doubled in value. So now, we have a lot that is paid for; the equity in the lot has doubled, and we are continuing to build equity in our existing home. God led us to a Christian builder that builds award-winning, custom homes who is working within our budget. In 18 to 24 months, we will walk into our new home with NO MORTGAGE! That is God!

The Lord is saying, "FOR YOUR SAKE, PLEASE TAKE THE LIMITS OFF OF ME."

Notes

Chapter Five

Walking In The Promises

ou will have to war in the Spirit to receive the promises of God. The Children of Israel had to conquer seven nations to take over the land that flowed with milk and honey. Don't think for a minute that you will not encounter opposition. The good news is that no weapon formed against you shall prosper. (Isaiah 54:7) It may be formed and you may see it. It may be intimidating and deadly; it won't prosper. You may get wounded by it, but it won't prosper. It may shake you to the core of your foundation, but it will not prosper. It will challenge you and stretch you, but it will not overtake you. This is God's promise to us. Satan is an already defeated foe. He was defeated over two thousand years ago on Calvary by our Lord and Savior, ___

Jesus Christ. The only way that we can forfeit our victory is by turning back and quitting. The enemy knows that the only way that he can cause us to lose is to cause us to quit fighting. We must fight the good fight of faith to achieve excellence in God.

We must be strong and very courageous.

We Must Focus on Our Focus.
Being Led by God

Joshua 3:1–4
1:And Joshua rose early in the morning; and they removed from Shit´-tim, and came to Jordan, he and all the children of Israel, and lodged there before they passed over. 2: And it came to pass after three days, that the officers went through the host; 3: And they commanded the people, saying, When ye see the ark of the covenant of the Lord your God, and the priests the Levites bearing it, then ye shall remove from your place, and go after it. 4: Yet there shall be a space between you and it, about two thousand cubits by measure: come not near unto it, that ye may know the way by which ye must go: for ye have not passed [this] way heretofore.

Before moving forward into the promised land,

the Children of Israel sanctified themselves. They prepared themselves for the march into the promises of God by first seeking His face. They were then commanded to move when they saw the Ark of the Covenant move. Christians, move when you see God move! Verse 4 lets us know not to get so far behind that we don't see God. Don't get slothful in your prayer life, in your reading, fasting, and devotional time that when God is leading you to make a right turn in a decision-making process that you don't see Him when He does. Also, don't get ahead of God. Don't become impatient and begin to attempt to make decisions and take actions without His guidance. Stay at a distance so you can see God move, because the place that you are going . . . "you have not passed this way before." The Lord is going to lead you into some territory that is unfamiliar to you. As you are led into His promises, don't be disturbed when you encounter things that you have never encountered before. Just keep you eyes on Him. The enemy wants to get you to take your eyes off of God for just an instant so that you will lose sight of Him. Satan wants to send a trial or snare your way to get you to look down or to the side, just for a blink, so that you can find yourself focusing on the problem and not the movement of God.

The Lord will prepare you and lead you in His plan for your life. He may not tell you what, specifically, you will encounter, but you will know when to prepare. I recall God speaking to me through a series of dreams. I had these dreams in a period of about one month. The basis of these dreams was very real. In each dream, I was with my family. We were in various places, sometimes in the city, sometimes in the fields of the country. Each time, wherever we were, tornadoes were dropping out of the horizon like paratroopers at an enemy invasion. As they got closer, I could hear and feel the noise and wind that they generated. I could feel the destructive power of their force. As my family and I huddled together holding one another, the Lord spoke to me in a quiet and peaceful voice that I could hear clearly over all of the mayhem. He simply told me to close my eyes and listen to His voice, and He would order my steps. I sincerely believe that the Lord told me to close my eyes because the overwhelming sight of these huge destructive forces would hinder my obeying His voice. As the tornadoes came, God would order each step I took. He would tell me to take two steps to the right and one forward. And I would hear the massive force just miss. I could hear the people screaming around me, being sucked up by the incredible funnel of mass destruction. Each dream had a different setting, but the result was the same. People were being destroyed all around us, and God was ordering our steps, even to the point of Him telling me in one dream not to move at all from an incoming twister. When it was an arms-length distance away, it dissipated. What was God telling me? He was letting me know that I was going to encounter some heavy wickedness that would come to distract and destroy, so I must be in tune to His voice. Don't look at your surroundings, listen for God's voice.

Joshua Meant Business

The Children of Israel lost a battle to the nation of A´-i. (Joshua Chapter 7)

During their battles to enter into the promises of God, the Children of Israel lost a battle. This battle was lost because of disobedience and sin in their camp. Immediately after the loss, Joshua went to God and found out the cause. It was revealed that Achan, the son of Carmi, had sinned against God by stealing. What was the consequence? Achan and all of his family were stoned, burned, and buried along with all of their possessions. We must be focused when pursing the promises of God. Any relationship that hinders us in our battles, we must terminate.

Joshua does not sound like a man that took obtaining the promises of God lightly. We must have that same zeal in the Spirit.

Move unfruitful relationships out of your life. Jesus once cursed a fig tree because it did not bring forth any fruit. (Mark 11:21) The tree was in season and looked green, but it did not bring forth any fruit. What is the Lord telling us? . . . that it is not enough to look like a Christian and be perceived to be a Christian, but not bear any fruit. I don't care what people claim or even look like. Where is the fruit? Fruitless people only serve to drain the resources and life out of those that are fruitful. Any tree that doesn't bring forth fruit is hewn down and cast into the fire. Let's face the fact that everyone is not going to enter into the promises of God. Every one of the Children of Israel did not enter into the promised land. You must "guard your anointing."

Let's learn from Abraham. The Lord told Abraham to get out from among his kindred. Abraham took Lot with him anyway. Notice that Abraham did not enter into the promises of God until he separated himself from Lot. You must identify and take action on the Lot-type relationships in your life, those that are unfruitful. Lot represents people that are disobedient, selfish, slothful, complacent, unmotivated, and codependent. I have found myself in both business and personal relationships that I was giving to the point of expectancy by the other party. It was a never-ending vacuum of one-sided giving. It seemed like the more I gave the more the receiving party expected me to give. I understand that those that are strong should bear the infirmities of those that are weak. (Romans 15:7) It is when the recipients of your help begin to look to you and not God as their source that immediate action must be taken. You are then in the position of becoming a stumbling block. Again, without question, we are helpers to one another. However, if someone is walking in disobedience to God's will for his or her life, the best thing to do is to put some distance in that relationship so that God can deal with it.

If you are going to create lasting change in your life, there are certain relationships that are directly associated with the behavior that you are attempting to alter. Relationships produce behavior in an association and cause-effect manner. Remember, that evil communication corrupts good manners. (I Corinthians 15:33) What we want to do is create and develop relationships that produce positive and fruitful behavior. Don't settle to be weighed down by negative people that constantly erode your positive outlook or self-esteem.

The Fruit of the Land

When you come out of your season of testing, God renews you with a new anointing so that you will not keep the mentality of a trial season. You will bring forth a fresh anointing that permeates the fellowship of His suffering and the power of His resurrection. You will understand what it means to be broken, yet you will know that He is able to keep you. Your faith will be stronger. And your fellowship with Him closer. Let the power of God rest upon you as He elevates you to a new spiritual level. The Lord is speaking to someone even as you read. "Now" is what He is saying. Not later, not soon, not wait, but now! No more manna. No more day-to-day making it. It's time for you to eat of the fruit of the promise. Remember, in the book of Joshua 5:12, it says: "And the manna ceased on the morrow after they had eaten of the old corn of the land; neither had the Children of Israel manna any more; but they did eat of the fruit of the land of Canaan that year." When you get to that place in God that you are walking in His promises, you will then find yourself no longer living from hand to mouth, paycheck to paycheck, and beneath your means. It does not, I warn you, negate the fact that the just shall live by faith. You will, however, find yourself with different trials. Remember, trials (processes) are the road to your blessings. It doesn't make sense naturally, and it certainly doesn't feel good to our flesh. I can hear the Lord saying in the Spirit, "GOOD." It's not supposed to feel good. It is supposed to mortify that which is not like Me. The heat is supposed to incinerate everything that needs to be seared out of your life. When I'm done, you will look more like Me, talk more like Me, act, behave, give, help others more like Me. The blessings that God has for you will be brought forth under the furnace and fining pot (Proverbs 17:3) so that you will be well fit for them.

List the unfruitful relationships in your life and rectify them either by modifying or removing them.

L I S T

Unfruitful Relationships

☜

_____

_____

_____

_____

_____

_____

_____

_____

_____

_____

_____

_____

_____

_____

_____

_____

_____

_____

_____

_____

_____

Blessings and Curses

Deuteronomy 28:1–14

1: And it shall come to pass, if thou shalt hearken diligently unto the voice of the Lord thy God, to observe [and] to do all his commandments which I command thee this day, that the Lord thy God will set thee on high above all nations of the earth: 2: And all these blessings shall come on thee, and overtake thee, if thou shalt hearken unto the voice of the lord thy God. 3: Blessed [shalt] thou [be] in the city, and blessed [shalt] thou [be] in the field. 4: Blessed [shall be] the fruit of thy body, and the fruit of thy ground, and the fruit of thy cattle, the increase of thy kine, and the flocks of thy sheep. 5: Blessed [shall be] thy basket and thy store. 6: Blessed [shalt] thou [be] when thou comest in, and blessed [shalt] thou [be] when thou goest out. 7: The Lord shall cause thine enemies that rise up against thee to be smitten before thy face: they shall come out against thee one way, and flee before thee seven ways. 8: The Lord shall command the blessing upon thee in thy storehouses, and in all that thou settest thine hand unto; and he shall bless thee in the land which the Lord thy God giveth thee. 9: The Lord shall establish thee a holy people unto himself, as he hath sworn unto thee, if thou shalt keep the commandments of the Lord thy God, and walk in his ways. 10: And all people of the earth shall see that thou art called by the name of the Lord; and they shall be afraid of thee. 11: And the Lord shall make thee plenteous in goods, in the fruit of thy body, and in the fruit of thy cattle, and in the fruit of thy ground, in the land which the Lord sware unto thy fathers to give thee. 12: The Lord shall open unto thee his good treasure, the heaven to give the rain unto thy land in his season, and to bless all the work of thine hand: and thou shalt lend unto many nations, and thou shalt not borrow. 13: And the Lord shall make thee the head, and not the tail; and thou shalt be above only, and thou shalt not be beneath; if that thou hearken unto the commandments of the Lord thy God, which I command thee this day, to observe and to do [them]: 14: And thou shalt not go aside from any of the words which I command thee this day, [to] the right hand, or [to] the left, to go after other gods to serve them.

It shall come to pass. The scripture in verse 1 does not say it might come to pass or it is a strong possibility that it will come to pass. It is stating that the blessings that the Lord has outlined in versus 2 through13 are already instituted and established if we "hearken diligently" to His voice, and observe and to do all His commandments. God is establishing a covenant with us. The word hearken means to understand and to be obedient. To unleash Godly blessings, we must know God's Word and understand what it is telling us to do. We error not knowing the scriptures, and we perish for a lack of knowledge. You must study the Word of God for yourself. What you've heard others say that it says is not sufficient. So many times we quote what we hear other people quote. Most of the time when you do this you get a quandary of cross quoting, intersecting, and an out-of-context fusion of scripture. You get sound-bite teaching and preaching to fit a particular point that is trying to be made. Friend, you better get into the Word of God for yourself . . . Study to show thyself approved unto God . . . (II Timothy 2:15)

We must also know His voice before we can be obedient to it. What does this tell us? It is back to the relationship. You must talk to God, and, more importantly, let Him talk to you. The more you talk with God, the more you hear His voice. The more you hear His voice the more distinguishable it is to you. The closer He is to you in relationship, the clearer He sounds when He speaks to you. Think naturally. If someone is a block away, they are barely audible to you. If someone is whispering in your ear, the more clear they sound.

I recall hearing the story of a mother walking through her home calling her son. She was telling him to wake up or he would be late for school. "Johnny, wake up or you will be late for school." She got no response, so she went up to his room and yelled again for him to "rise and shine" for school. Johnny, groggily, turned to his mother with one eye still closed and said, "Mother I don't want to go to school this morning. Nobody there likes me. Out of all the kids in that school, I can't think of one that likes me. Out of all of the teachers in that school, I can't think of one that likes me. Mother, give me one good reason why I should go to school this morning." His mother said, "I'll give you two good reasons. The first one is that you are thirty-five years old. The second is that you are the principal." This story may sound amusing, but it does illustrate the fact that studies have shown that 80 percent of the people in the work force in the United States do not enjoy their jobs. This is a major driving force behind the lack of excellence in performance. Face it, if you don't like what you are doing, you will not spend the time nor energy necessary to excel at it. On the other hand, if you like an activity, you will spend time to develop your skills in that area.

Once while speaking at a seminar, I asked the participants to give me synonyms and adjectives that they associated with their job. Most of the responses were typical: "boring," "tiring"; endure and dislike are the general tone. Some outright said that they did not like their jobs nor the challenges presented to them there. I asked them, "Why, if you see your workplace as simply as the place to go to endure trials, do you continue to subject yourselves to it? Why do you go to a job that undermines your very spiritual existence? Why have you allowed your soul to outgrow your job?" The overwhelming response was, "It pays the bills." Our spiritual man is hungering and thirsting to be challenged to the very brink of its capacity, and as far as we can get is "paying the bills."

Your Passion and God's Purpose

When you find yourself in a position that the passion that you have is aligned with God's purpose for your life, then you will find yourself prospering. Your passion is that inner drive that causes you to throw yourself into and diligently pursue its fulfillment — that thing that you do that causes fulfillment and completeness. When passion is aligned with purpose, watch out! You mean you can actually enjoy doing the will of God? You can actually find yourself being blessed, just by finding the divine purpose for your life and then yielding to the Holy Spirit to fill you with the desire to fulfill it? That is incredible! Our old passions are not divine. They are carnal and must be mortified. Once you allow the Lord to lead and guide you into purpose, He will equip you with the gifts, talent, and, yes, the passion to fulfill His will. Do not try to figure this out; only yield. Only be willing and obedient. God, almighty, will change your appetites. He will remove the taste of sin's bondage from your mouth. He will extract desires that have been buried deep in the inner most parts of your soul. Then He will replace them with His purpose, will, and of course power.

It is my prayer that you have been inspired into action to begin Unleashing the Blessings of God in YOUR life!

Notes

Notes

Notes

Notes

Notes

Notes

Notes

Notes